Edited by Jessie B. Rittenhouse

THE LITTLE BOOK OF AMERICAN POETS.
THE LITTLE BOOK OF MODERN VERSE.

HOUGHTON MIFFLIN COMPANY
BOSTON AND NEW YORK

THE LITTLE BOOK OF MODERN VERSE

THE LITTLE BOOK OF MODERN VERSE

A
SELECTION FROM THE WORK
OF CONTEMPORANEOUS
AMERICAN POETS

EDITED BY
JESSIE B. RITTENHOUSE
Author of "The Younger American Poets," etc.

BOSTON AND NEW YORK
HOUGHTON MIFFLIN COMPANY
The Riverside Press Cambridge

Published October 1913

FOREWORD

"THE LITTLE BOOK OF MODERN VERSE," as its name implies, is not a formal anthology. The pageant of American poetry has been so often presented that no necessity exists for another exhaustive review of the art. Nearly all anthologies, however, stop short of the present group of poets, or represent them so inadequately that only those in close touch with the trend of American literature know what the poet of to-day is contributing to it.

It is strictly, then, as a reflection of our own period, to show what is being done by the successors of our earlier poets, what new interpretation they are giving to life, what new beauty they have apprehended, what new art they have evolved, that this little book has taken form. A few of the poets included have been writing for a quarter of a century, and were, therefore, among the immediate successors of the New England group, but many have done their work within the past decade and the volume as a whole represents the twentieth-century spirit.

From the scheme of the book, that of a small, intimate collection, representative rather than exhaustive, it has been impossible to include all of the poets who would naturally be included in a more ambitious anthology. In certain instances, also, matters of copyright have deterred me from including those whom I had originally intended to represent, but with isolated exceptions the little book covers the work of our later poets and gives a hint of what they are doing.

I have attempted, as far as possible, to unify the collection by arranging the poems so that each should set the keynote to the next, or at least bear some relation to it in mood or theme. While it is impossible, with so varied a mass of material, that such a sequence should be exact, and in one or two instances the arrangement has been disturbed by the late addition or elimination of poems, the idea has been to differentiate the little volume from the typical anthology by giving it a unity impossible to a larger collection.

JESSIE B. RITTENHOUSE.

CONTENTS

ACKNOWLEDGMENTS

THANKS are due to the following publishers for permission to include selections from the volumes enumerated below: —

To Messrs. Houghton Mifflin Co. for selections from "Poems and Poetic Dramas," by William Vaughn Moody; "Happy Ending," by Louise Imogen Guiney; "Uriel, and Other Poems," by Percy MacKaye; "A Troop of the Guard," by Hermann Hagedorn; "Poems and Poetic Dramas," by George Cabot Lodge; "Little Gray Songs from St. Joseph's," by Grace Fallow Norton; "Poems and Poetic Dramas," by Trumbull Stickney; "Scum o' the Earth," by Robert Haven Schauffler; "The Inverted Torch," by Edith M. Thomas; "The Ride to the Lady, and Other Poems," and "Oberon and Puck," by Helen Gray Cone; "The Singing Man," and "The Singing Leaves," by Josephine Preston Peabody; "The Shoes that Danced, and Other Poems," by Anna Hempstead Branch; "The Unconquered Air," "Lyrics of Life," and "Poems," by Florence Earle Coates; "Lyrics of Joy," by Frank Dempster Sherman; "Poems," by John Vance Cheney; "A Quiet Road," by Lizette Woodworth Reese; "A Dome of Many-Coloured Glass," by Amy Lowell; and for the following poems from the *Atlantic Monthly:* "On a Subway Express," by Chester Firkins; "Evensong," and "The Lesser Children," by Ridgely Torrence.

To Messrs. Charles Scribner's Sons for selections from "The Town down the River," by Edwin Arlington Robinson; "A Winter Swallow," by Edith M. Thomas; "Poems," by Josephine Dodge Daskam; and from *Scribner's Magazine:* "A Memorial Tablet," by Florence Wilkinson, and "Comrades," by George Edward Woodberry.

To Messrs. Doubleday, Page & Co. for selections from "The Man with the Hoe, and Other Poems," and "Lincoln, and Other Poems," by Edwin Markham; "The Far Country," by Florence Wilkinson; "Many Gods," and "Far Quests," by Cale Young Rice; and "A Summer of Love," by Joyce Kilmer.

To Lothrop, Lee & Shepard Co. for selections from "Message and Melody," "Lyrics of Brotherhood," and "Dumb in June," by Richard Burton.

To Messrs. Dana Estes & Co. for selections from "Love Triumphant," and "On Life's Stairway," by Frederic Lawrence Knowles.

To Messrs. Duffield & Co. for selections from "The Frozen Grail, and Other Poems," and "The Book of Love," by Elsa Barker; "Poems," by George Santayana; and "Along the Trail," by Richard Hovey.

To Messrs. L. C. Page & Co. for selections from "Poems: New Complete Edition," by Charles G. D. Roberts, copyright, 1903, and "The Green Book of the Bards," by Bliss Carman, copyright, 1903.

To A. M. Robertson for selections from "A Wine of Wizardry," and "The House of Orchids," by George Sterling, and "Poems," by Nora May French.

To S. S. McClure Co. for the use of the poem "There's Rosemary," by Olive Tilford Dargan, published in *McClure's Magazine.*

To Messrs. Small, Maynard & Co. for selections from "Songs from Vagabondia," "More Songs from Vagabondia," and "Last Songs from Vagabondia," by Bliss Carman and Richard Hovey; "An Ode to Harvard, and Other Poems," by Witter Bynner; and "The Poet, the Fool, and the Fairies," by Madison Cawein.

To The John Lane Co. for selections from "New Poems," and "English Poems," by Richard Le Gallienne, and "Carmina," by Thomas Augustine Daly.

To The Century Co. for the use of the poems "When I have

gone Weird Ways," by John G. Neihardt, and "Chavez," by Mildred McNeal Sweeney.

To Thomas B. Mosher for selections from "A Wayside Lute," by Lizette Woodworth Reese.

To Messrs. G. P. Putnam's Sons for selections from "Helen of Troy, and Other Poems," by Sara Teasdale, and "Poems," by Robert Cameron Rogers.

To Messrs. Moffat, Yard & Co. for selections from "The Candle and the Flame," by George Sylvester Viereck.

To Messrs. Harper & Bros. for the use of the poems, "Azrael," by Robert Gilbert Welsh; "Frost To-night," by Edith M. Thomas; "Mother," by Theresa Helburn; and "May is building her House," by Richard Le Gallienne.

To The Bobbs-Merrill Company for the use of the following poems by James Whitcomb Riley: "The Rival," from "Green Fields and Running Brooks," copyrighted in 1892; "The Parting Guest" from "Morning," copyrighted in 1907.

To Mitchell Kennerley for selections from "A Quiet Singer," and "Youth," by Charles Hanson Towne; "The Joy o' Life," by Theodosia Garrison; "The Stranger at the Gate," by John G. Neihardt; for the use of "The Sea-Lands," by Orrick Johns, and "Sentence," by Witter Bynner, published in the *Forum;* and for "Renascence," by Edna St. Vincent Millay, and "He whom a Dream hath possessed," by Shaemas O Sheel, published in the *Lyric Year.*

To The Oxford University Press for selections from "Sonnets," by Lloyd Mifflin.

To Messrs. Henry Holt & Co. for selections from "Harps hung up in Babylon," by Arthur Colton.

To The Macmillan Co. for the use of selections from the "Collected Poems of George E. Woodberry"; and from "Myself and I," by Fannie Stearns Davis.

To George William Browning for the use of poems by Thomas S. Jones, Jr., and Clinton Scollard.

To Messrs. Sherman, French & Co. for selections from

"First Love," by Louis Untermeyer, and "The Beloved Adventure," by John Hall Wheelock.

To the *American Magazine* for the use of the poem "On the Building of Springfield," by Nicholas Vachel Lindsay.

To the *Smart Set* for the use of the sonnet, "A Faun in Wall Street," by John Myers O'Hara.

To Miss Harriet Monroe, editor of *Poetry*, for the use of "The Mystic," by Witter Bynner.

To William Stanley Braithwaite, editor of the *Poetry Journal*, for the use of "The Only Way," by Louis V. Ledoux.

To Messrs. John W. Luce & Co. for selections from "The House of Falling Leaves," by William Stanley Braithwaite.

To the editors of the *Outlook* for permission to reprint "Night's Mardi Gras," by Edward J. Wheeler.

Sincere thanks are due also to my friend Thomas S. Jones, Jr., who, during my absence in Europe, has kindly taken charge of all details incident to putting "The Little Book of Modern Verse" through the press.

THE LITTLE BOOK OF MODERN VERSE

LORD OF MY HEART'S ELATION

LORD of my heart's elation,
Spirit of things unseen,
Be thou my aspiration
Consuming and serene!

Bear up, bear out, bear onward,
This mortal soul alone,
To selfhood or oblivion,
Incredibly thine own, —

As the foamheads are loosened
And blown along the sea,
Or sink and merge forever
In that which bids them be.

I, too, must climb in wonder,
Uplift at thy command, —
Be one with my frail fellows
Beneath the wind's strong hand,

A fleet and shadowy column
Of dust or mountain rain,
To walk the earth a moment
And be dissolved again.

Be thou my exaltation
Or fortitude of mien,
Lord of the world's elation,
Thou breath of things unseen!

Bliss Carman.

GLOUCESTER MOORS

A MILE behind is Gloucester town
Where the fishing fleets put in,
A mile ahead the land dips down
And the woods and farms begin.
Here, where the moors stretch free
In the high blue afternoon,
Are the marching sun and talking sea,
And the racing winds that wheel and flee
On the flying heels of June.

Jill-o'er-the-ground is purple blue,
Blue is the quaker-maid,
The wild geranium holds its dew
Long in the boulder's shade.
Wax-red hangs the cup
From the huckleberry boughs,
In barberry bells the grey moths sup
Or where the choke-cherry lifts high up
Sweet bowls for their carouse.

Over the shelf of the sandy cove
Beach-peas blossom late.
By copse and cliff the swallows rove
Each calling to his mate.
Seaward the sea-gulls go,
And the land-birds all are here;
That green-gold flash was a vireo,
And yonder flame where the marsh-flags grow
Was a scarlet tanager.

This earth is not the steadfast place
We landsmen build upon;

From deep to deep she varies pace,
And while she comes is gone.
Beneath my feet I feel
Her smooth bulk heave and dip;
With velvet plunge and soft upreel
She swings and steadies to her keel
Like a gallant, gallant ship.

These summer clouds she sets for sail,
The sun is her masthead light,
She tows the moon like a pinnace frail
Where her phosphor wake churns bright.
Now hid, now looming clear,
On the face of the dangerous blue
The star fleets tack and wheel and veer,
But on, but on does the old earth steer
As if her port she knew.

God, dear God! Does she know her port,
Though she goes so far about?
Or blind astray, does she make her sport
To brazen and chance it out?
I watched when her captains passed:
She were better captainless.
Men in the cabin, before the mast,
But some were reckless and some aghast,
And some sat gorged at mess.

By her battened hatch I leaned and caught
Sounds from the noisome hold, —
Cursing and sighing of souls distraught
And cries too sad to be told.
Then I strove to go down and see;
But they said, "Thou art not of us!"

I turned to those on the deck with me
And cried, "Give help!" But they said, "Let be:
Our ship sails faster thus."

Jill-o'er-the-ground is purple blue,
Blue is the quaker-maid,
The alder-clump where the brook comes through
Breeds cresses in its shade.
To be out of the moiling street
With its swelter and its sin!
Who has given to me this sweet,
And given my brother dust to eat?
And when will his wage come in?

Scattering wide or blown in ranks,
Yellow and white and brown,
Boats and boats from the fishing banks
Come home to Gloucester town.
There is cash to purse and spend,
There are wives to be embraced,
Hearts to borrow and hearts to lend,
And hearts to take and keep to the end, —
O little sails, make haste!

But thou, vast outbound ship of souls,
What harbor town for thee?
What shapes, when thy arriving tolls,
Shall crowd the banks to see?
Shall all the happy shipmates then
Stand singing brotherly?
Or shall a haggard ruthless few
Warp her over and bring her to,
While the many broken souls of men

Fester down in the slaver's pen,
And nothing to say or do?
William Vaughn Moody.

ON A SUBWAY EXPRESS

I, WHO have lost the stars, the sod,
For chilling pave and cheerless light,
Have made my meeting-place with God
A new and nether Night —

Have found a fane where thunder fills
Loud caverns, tremulous; — and these
Atone me for my reverend hills
And moonlit silences.

A figment in the crowded dark,
Where men sit muted by the roar,
I ride upon the whirring Spark
Beneath the city's floor.

In this dim firmament, the stars
Whirl by in blazing files and tiers;
Kin meteors graze our flying bars,
Amid the spinning spheres.

Speed! speed! until the quivering rails
Flash silver where the head-light gleams,
As when on lakes the Moon impales
The waves upon its beams.

Life throbs about me, yet I stand
Outgazing on majestic Power;

Death rides with me, on either hand,
  In my communion hour.

You that 'neath country skies can pray,
  Scoff not at me — the city clod; —
My only respite of the Day
  Is this wild ride — with God.

Chester Firkins.

THE AUTOMOBILE

FLUID the world flowed under us: the hills
  Billow on billow of umbrageous green
  Heaved us, aghast, to fresh horizons, seen
One rapturous instant, blind with flash of rills
And silver-rising storms and dewy stills
  Of dripping boulders, till the dim ravine
  Drowned us again in leafage, whose serene
Coverts grew loud with our tumultuous wills.

Then all of Nature's old amazement seemed
  Sudden to ask us: "Is this also Man?
  This plunging, volant, land-amphibian
What Plato mused and Paracelsus dreamed?
  Reply!" And piercing us with ancient scan,
The shrill, primeval hawk gazed down — and screamed.

Percy MacKaye.

THE BLACK VULTURE

ALOOF upon the day's immeasured dome,
  He holds unshared the silence of the sky.
  Far down his bleak, relentless eyes descry

The eagle's empire and the falcon's home —
Far down, the galleons of sunset roam;
His hazards on the sea of morning lie;
Serene, he hears the broken tempest sigh
Where cold sierras gleam like scattered foam.

And least of all he holds the human swarm —
Unwitting now that envious men prepare
To make their dream and its fulfillment one,
When, poised above the caldrons of the storm,
Their hearts, contemptuous of death, shall dare
His roads between the thunder and the sun.

George Sterling.

CHAVEZ

So hath he fallen, the Endymion of the air,
And so lies down in slumber lapped for aye.
Diana, passing, found his youth too fair,
His soul too fleet and willing to obey.
She swung her golden moon before his eyes —
Dreaming, he rose to follow — and ran — and was away.

His foot was wingèd as the mounting sun.
Earth he disdained — the dusty ways of men
Not yet had learned. His spirit longed to run
With the bright clouds, his brothers, to answer when
The airs were fleetest and could give him hand
Into the starry fields beyond our plodding ken.

All wittingly that glorious way he chose,
And loved the peril when it was most bright.

He tried anew the long-forbidden snows
And like an eagle topped the dropping height
Of Nagenhorn, and still toward Italy
Past peak and cliff pressed on, in glad, unerring flight.

Oh, when the bird lies low with golden wing
Bruisèd past healing by some bitter chance,
Still must its tireless spirit mount and sing
Of meadows green with morning, of the dance
On windy trees, the darting flight away,
And of that last, most blue, triumphant downward glance.

So murmuring of the snow: "*The snow, and more,
O God, more snow!*" on that last field he lay.
Despair and wonder spent their passsionate store
In his great heart, through heaven gone astray,
And early lost. Too far the golden moon
Had swung upon that bright, that long, untraversed way.

Now to lie ended on the murmuring plain —
Ah, this for his bold heart was not the loss,
But that those windy fields he ne'er again
Might try, nor fleet and shimmering mountains cross,
Unfollowed, by a path none other knew:
His bitter woe had here its deep and piteous cause.

Dear toils of youth unfinished! And songs unwritten, left
By young and passionate hearts! O melodies
Unheard, whereof we ever stand bereft!
Clear-singing Schubert, boyish Keats — with these

He roams henceforth, one with the starry band,
  Still paying to fairy call and far command
His spirit heed, still winged with golden prophecies.

Mildred McNeal Sweeney.

THE SEA GYPSY

I am fevered with the sunset,
I am fretful with the bay,
For the wander-thirst is on me
And my soul is in Cathay.

There 's a schooner in the offing,
With her topsails shot with fire,
And my heart has gone aboard her
For the Islands of Desire.

I must forth again to-morrow!
With the sunset I must be
Hull down on the trail of rapture
In the wonder of the sea.

Richard Hovey.

AT GIBRALTAR

I

England, I stand on thy imperial ground,
Not all a stranger; as thy bugles blow,
I feel within my blood old battles flow —
The blood whose ancient founts in thee are found.
Still surging dark against the Christian bound
Wide Islam presses; well its peoples know

Thy heights that watch them wandering below;
I think how Lucknow heard their gathering sound.
I turn, and meet the cruel, turbaned face.
England, 't is sweet to be so much thy son!
I feel the conqueror in my blood and race;
Last night Trafalgar awed me, and to-day
Gibraltar wakened; hark, thy evening gun
Startles the desert over Africa!

II

Thou art the rock of empire, set mid-seas
Between the East and West, that God has built;
Advance thy Roman borders where thou wilt,
While run thy armies true with His decrees.
Law, justice, liberty — great gifts are these;
Watch that they spread where English blood is spilt,
Lest, mixed and sullied with his country's guilt,
The soldier's life-stream flow, and Heaven displease!
Two swords there are: one naked, apt to smite,
Thy blade of war; and, battle-storied, one
Rejoices in the sheath, and hides from light.
American I am; would wars were done!
Now westward, look, my country bids good-night —
Peace to the world from ports without a gun!

George Edward Woodberry.

EUCHENOR CHORUS

(*From "The City"*)

Of old it went forth to Euchenor, pronounced of his
sire —
Reluctant, impelled by the god's unescapable fire —

To choose for his doom or to perish at home of disease
Or be slain of his foes, among men, where Troy surges down to the seas.

Polyides, the soothsayer, spake it, inflamed by the god.
Of his son whom the fates singled out did he bruit it abroad;
And Euchenor went down to the ships with his armor and men
And straightway, grown dim on the gulf, passed the isles he passed never again.

Why weep ye, O women of Corinth? The doom ye have heard
Is it strange to your ears that ye make it so mournful a word?
Is he who so fair in your eyes to his manhood upgrew,
Alone in his doom of pale death — are of mortals the beaten so few?

O weep not, companions and lovers! Turn back to your joys:
The defeat was not his which he chose, nor the victory Troy's.
Him a conqueror, beauteous in youth, o'er the flood his fleet brought,
And the swift spear of Paris that slew completed the conquest he sought.

Not the falling proclaims the defeat, but the place of the fall;
And the fate that decrees and the god that impels through it all

Regard not blind mortals' divisions of slayer and slain,
But invisible glories dispense wide over the war-gleaming plain.

Arthur Upson.

HE WHOM A•DREAM HATH POSSESSED

He whom a dream hath possessed knoweth no more of doubting,
For mist and the blowing of winds and the mouthing of words he scorns;
Not the sinuous speech of schools he hears, but a knightly shouting,
And never comes darkness down, yet he greeteth a million morns.

He whom a dream hath possessed knoweth no more of roaming;
All roads and the flowing of waves and the speediest flight he knows,
But wherever his feet are set, his soul is forever homing,
And going, he comes, and coming he heareth a call and goes.

He whom a dream hath possessed knoweth no more of sorrow,
At death and the dropping of leaves and the fading of suns he smiles,
For a dream remembers no past and scorns the desire of a morrow,
And a dream in a sea of doom sets surely the ultimate isles.

He whom a dream hath possessed treads the impalpable marches,
From the dust of the day's long road he leaps to a laughing star,
And the ruin of worlds that fall he views from eternal arches,
And rides God's battlefield in a flashing and golden car.

Shaemas O Sheel.

THE KINGS

A MAN said unto his Angel:
"My spirits are fallen low,
And I cannot carry this battle:
O brother! where might I go?

"The terrible Kings are on me
With spears that are deadly bright;
Against me so from the cradle
Do fate and my fathers fight."

Then said to the man his Angel:
"Thou wavering, witless soul,
Back to the ranks! What matter
To win or to lose the whole,

"As judged by the little judges
Who hearken not well, nor see?
Not thus, by the outer issue,
The Wise shall interpret thee.

"Thy will is the sovereign measure
And only events of things:

The puniest heart, defying,
Were stronger than all these Kings.

"Though out of the past they gather,
Mind's Doubt, and Bodily Pain,
And pallid Thirst of the Spirit
That is kin to the other twain,

"And Grief, in a cloud of banners,
And ringletted Vain Desires,
And Vice, with the spoils upon him
Of thee and thy beaten sires, —

"While Kings of eternal evil
Yet darken the hills about,
Thy part is with broken sabre
To rise on the last redoubt;

"To fear not sensible failure,
Nor covet the game at all,
But fighting, fighting, fighting,
Die, driven against the wall."

Louise Imogen Guiney.

MOCKERY

God, I return to You on April days
When along country roads You walk with me,
And my faith blossoms like the earliest tree
That shames the bleak world with its yellow sprays —
My faith revives, when through a rosy haze
The clover-sprinkled hills smile quietly,
Young winds uplift a bird's clean ecstasy . . .
For this, O God, my joyousness and praise!

But now — the crowded streets and choking airs,
    The squalid people, bruised and tossed about;
These, or the over-brilliant thoroughfares,
    The too-loud laughter and the empty shout,
The mirth-mad city, tragic with its cares . . .
    For this, O God, my silence — and my doubt.

Louis Untermeyer.

AN ODE IN TIME OF HESITATION

I

Before the solemn bronze Saint Gaudens made
To thrill the heedless passer's heart with awe,
And set here in the city's talk and trade
To the good memory of Robert Shaw,
This bright March morn I stand,
And hear the distant spring come up the land;
Knowing that what I hear is not unheard
Of this boy soldier and his Negro band,
For all their gaze is fixed so stern ahead,
For all the fatal rhythm of their tread.
The land they died to save from death and shame
Trembles and waits, hearing the spring's great name,
And by her pangs these resolute ghosts are stirred.

II

Through street and mall the tides of people go
Heedless; the trees upon the Common show
No hint of green; but to my listening heart
The still earth doth impart
Assurance of her jubilant emprise,
And it is clear to my long-searching eyes

That love at last has might upon the skies.
The ice is runneled on the little pond;
A telltale patter drips from off the trees;
The air is touched with Southland spiceries,
As if but yesterday it tossed the frond
Of pendant mosses where the live-oaks grow
Beyond Virginia and the Carolines,
Or had its will among the fruits and vines
Of aromatic isles asleep beyond
Florida and the Gulf of Mexico.

III

Soon shall the Cape Ann children shout in glee,
Spying the arbutus, spring's dear recluse;
Hill lads at dawn shall hearken the wild goose
Go honking northward over Tennessee;
West from Oswego to Sault Sainte-Marie,
And on to where the Pictured Rocks are hung,
And yonder where, gigantic, wilful, young,
Chicago sitteth at the northwest gates,
With restless violent hands and casual tongue
Moulding her mighty fates,
The Lakes shall robe them in ethereal sheen;
And like a larger sea, the vital green
Of springing wheat shall vastly be outflung
Over Dakota and the prairie states.
By desert people immemorial
On Arizonan mesas shall be done
Dim rites unto the thunder and the sun;
Nor shall the primal gods lack sacrifice
More splendid, when the white Sierras call
Unto the Rockies straightway to arise
And dance before the unveiled ark of the year.

Sounding their windy cedars as for shawms,
Unrolling rivers clear
For flutter of broad phylacteries;
While Shasta signals to Alaskan seas
That watch old sluggish glaciers downward creep
To fling their icebergs thundering from the steep,
And Mariposa through the purple calms
Gazes at far Hawaii crowned with palms
Where East and West are met, —
A rich seal on the ocean's bosom set
To say that East and West are twain,
With different loss and gain:
The Lord hath sundered them; let them be sundered
 yet.

IV

Alas! what sounds are these that come
Sullenly over the Pacific seas, —
Sounds of ignoble battle, striking dumb
The season's half-awakened ecstasies?
Must I be humble, then,
Now when my heart hath need of pride?
Wild love falls on me from these sculptured men;
By loving much the land for which they died
I would be justified.
My spirit was away on pinions wide
To soothe in praise of her its passionate mood
And ease it of its ache of gratitude.
Too sorely heavy is the debt they lay
On me and the companions of my day.
I would remember now
My country's goodliness, make sweet her name.
Alas! what shade art thou

Of sorrow or of blame
Liftest the lyric leafage from her brow,
And pointest a slow finger at her shame?

V

Lies! lies! It cannot be! The wars we wage
Are noble, and our battles still are won
By justice for us, ere we lift the gage.
We have not sold our loftiest heritage.
The proud republic hath not stooped to cheat
And scramble in the market-place of war;
Her forehead weareth yet its solemn star.
Here is her witness: this, her perfect son,
This delicate and proud New England soul
Who leads despisèd men, with just-unshackled feet,
Up the large ways where death and glory meet,
To show all peoples that our shame is done,
That once more we are clean and spirit-whole.

VI

Crouched in the sea-fog on the moaning sand
All night he lay, speaking some simple word
From hour to hour to the slow minds that heard,
Holding each poor life gently in his hand
And breathing on the base rejected clay
Till each dark face shone mystical and grand
Against the breaking day;
And lo, the shard the potter cast away
Was grown a fiery chalice crystal-fine,
Fulfilled of the divine
Great wine of battle wrath by God's ring-finger
stirred.

Then upward, where the shadowy bastion loomed
Huge on the mountain in the wet sea light,
Whence now, and now, infernal flowerage bloomed,
Bloomed, burst, and scattered down its deadly
seed, —
They swept, and died like freemen on the height,
Like freemen, and like men of noble breed;
And when the battle fell away at night
By hasty and contemptuous hands were thrust
Obscurely in a common grave with him
The fair-haired keeper of their love and trust.
Now limb doth mingle with dissolvèd limb
In nature's busy old democracy
To flush the mountain laurel when she blows
Sweet by the Southern sea,
And heart with crumbled heart climbs in the rose: —
The untaught hearts with the high heart that knew
This mountain fortress for no earthly hold
Of temporal quarrel, but the bastion old
Of spiritual wrong,
Built by an unjust nation sheer and strong,
Expugnable but by a nation's rue
And bowing down before that equal shrine
By all men held divine,
Whereof his band and he were the most holy sign.

VII

O bitter, bitter shade!
Wilt thou not put the scorn
And instant tragic question from thine eye?
Do thy dark brows yet crave
That swift and angry stave —
Unmeet for this desirous morn —

That I have striven, striven to evade?
Gazing on him, must I not deem they err
Whose careless lips in street and shop aver
As common tidings, deeds to make his cheek
Flush from the bronze, and his dead throat to speak?
Surely some elder singer would arise,
Whose harp hath leave to threaten and to mourn
Above this people when they go astray.
Is Whitman, the strong spirit, overworn?
Has Whittier put his yearning wrath away?
I will not and I dare not yet believe!
Though furtively the sunlight seems to grieve,
And the spring-laden breeze
Out of the gladdening west is sinister
With sounds of nameless battle overseas;
Though when we turn and question in suspense
If these things be indeed after these ways,
And what things are to follow after these,
Our fluent men of place and consequence
Fumble and fill their mouths with hollow phrase,
Or for the end-all of deep arguments
Intone their dull commercial liturgies —
I dare not yet believe! My ears are shut!
I will not hear the thin satiric praise
And muffled laughter of our enemies,
Bidding us never sheathe our valiant sword
Till we have changed our birthright for a gourd
Of wild pulse stolen from a barbarian's hut;
Showing how wise it is to cast away
The symbols of our spiritual sway,
That so our hands with better ease
May wield the driver's whip and grasp the jailer's keys.

VIII

Was it for this our fathers kept the law?
This crown shall crown their struggle and their ruth?
Are we the eagle nation Milton saw
Mewing its mighty youth,
Soon to possess the mountain winds of truth,
And be a swift familiar of the sun
Where aye before God's face his trumpets run?
Or have we but the talons and the maw,
And for the abject likeness of our heart
Shall some less lordly bird be set apart?
Some gross-billed wader where the swamps are fat?
Some gorger in the sun? Some prowler with the bat?

IX

Ah, no!
We have not fallen so.
We are our fathers' sons: let those who lead us know!
'T was only yesterday sick Cuba's cry
Came up the tropic wind, "Now help us, for we
die!"
Then Alabama heard,
And rising, pale, to Maine and Idaho
Shouted a burning word.
Proud state with proud impassioned state conferred,
And at the lifting of a hand sprang forth,
East, west, and south, and north,
Beautiful armies. Oh, by the sweet blood and young
Shed on the awful hill slope at San Juan,
By the unforgotten names of eager boys
Who might have tasted girl's love and been stung
With the old mystic joys

And starry griefs, now the spring nights come on,
But that the heart of youth is generous, —
We charge you, ye who lead us,
Breathe on their chivalry no hint of stain!
Turn not their new-world victories to gain!
One least leaf plucked for chaffer from the bays
Of their dear praise,
One jot of their pure conquest put to hire,
The implacable republic will require;
With clamor, in the glare and gaze of noon,
Or subtly, coming as a thief at night,
But surely, very surely, slow or soon
That insult deep we deeply will requite.
Tempt not our weakness, our cupidity!
For save we let the island men go free,
Those baffled and dislaureled ghosts
Will curse us from the lamentable coasts
Where walk the frustrate dead.
The cup of trembling shall be drainèd quite,
Eaten the sour bread of astonishment,
With ashes of the hearth shall be made white
Our hair, and wailing shall be in the tent;
Then on your guiltier head
Shall our intolerable self-disdain
Wreak suddenly its anger and its pain;
For manifest in that disastrous light
We shall discern the right
And do it, tardily. — O ye who lead,
Take heed!
Blindness we may forgive, but baseness we will smite.

William Vaughn Moody.

CANDLEMAS

O HEARKEN, all ye little weeds
That lie beneath the snow,
(So low, dear hearts, in poverty so low!)
The sun hath risen for royal deeds,
A valiant wind the vanguard leads;
Now quicken ye, lest unborn seeds
Before ye rise and blow.

O furry living things, adream
On winter's drowsy breast,
(How rest ye there, how softly, safely rest!)
Arise and follow where a gleam
Of wizard gold unbinds the stream,
And all the woodland windings seem
With sweet expectance blest.

My birds, come back! the hollow sky
Is weary for your note.
(Sweet-throat, come back! O liquid, mellow throat!)
Ere May's soft minions hereward fly,
Shame on ye, laggards, to deny
The brooding breast, the sun-bright eye,
The tawny, shining coat!

Alice Brown.

THE UNRETURNING

THE old eternal spring once more
Comes back the sad eternal way,
With tender rosy light before
The going-out of day.

The great white moon across my door
  A shadow in the twilight stirs;
But now forever comes no more
  That wondrous look of Hers.

Bliss Carman.

A SONG IN SPRING

O LITTLE buds all bourgeoning with Spring,
  You hold my winter in forgetfulness;
Without my window lilac branches swing,
Within my gate I hear a robin sing —
  O little laughing blooms that lift and bless!

So blow the breezes in a soft caress,
  Blowing my dreams upon a swallow's wing;
O little merry buds in dappled dress,
You fill my heart with very wantonness —
  O little buds all bourgeoning with Spring!

Thomas S. Jones, Jr.

MAY IS BUILDING HER HOUSE

MAY is building her house. With apple blooms
    She is roofing over the glimmering rooms;
Of the oak and the beech hath she builded its beams,
    And, spinning all day at her secret looms,
With arras of leaves each wind-swayed wall
She pictureth over, and peopleth it all
    With echoes and dreams,
    And singing of streams.

May is building her house. Of petal and blade,
Of the roots of the oak, is the flooring made,
With a carpet of mosses and lichen and clover,
Each small miracle over and over,
And tender, traveling green things strayed.

Her windows, the morning and evening star,
And her rustling doorways, ever ajar
With the coming and going
Of fair things blowing,
The thresholds of the four winds are.

May is building her house. From the dust of things
She is making the songs and the flowers and the wings;
From October's tossed and trodden gold
She is making the young year out of the old;
Yea: out of winter's flying sleet
She is making all the summer sweet,
And the brown leaves spurned of November's feet
She is changing back again to spring's.

Richard Le Gallienne.

HERE IS THE PLACE WHERE LOVELINESS KEEPS HOUSE

Here is the place where Loveliness keeps house,
Between the river and the wooded hills,
Within a valley where the Springtime spills
Her firstling wind-flowers under blossoming boughs:
Where Summer sits braiding her warm, white brows
With bramble-roses; and where Autumn fills
Her lap with asters; and old Winter frills

With crimson haw and hip his snowy blouse.
Here you may meet with Beauty. Here she sits
Gazing upon the moon, or all the day
Tuning a wood-thrush flute, remote, unseen:
Or when the storm is out, 't is she who flits
From rock to rock, a form of flying spray,
Shouting, beneath the leaves' tumultuous green.

Madison Cawein.

WATER FANTASY

O BROWN brook, O blithe brook, what will you say to me
If I take off my heavy shoon and wade you childishly?

O take them off, and come to me.
You shall not fall. Step merrily!

But, cool brook, but, quick brook, and what if I should float
White-bodied in your pleasant pool, your bubbles at my throat?

If you are but a mortal maid,
Then I shall make you half afraid.
The water shall be dim and deep,
And silver fish shall lunge and leap
About you, coward mortal thing.
But if you come desiring
To win once more your naiadhood,
How you shall laugh and find me good —
My golden surfaces, my glooms,
My secret grottoes' dripping rooms,

My depths of warm wet emerald,
My mosses floating fold on fold!
And where I take the rocky leap
Like wild white water shall you sweep;
Like wild white water shall you cry,
Trembling and turning to the sky,
While all the thousand-fringèd trees
Glimmer and glisten through the breeze.
I bid you come! Too long, too long,
You have forgot my undersong.
And this perchance you never knew:
E'en I, the brook, have need of you.
My naiads faded long ago, —
My little nymphs, that to and fro
Within my waters sunnily
Made small white flames of tinkling glee.
I have been lonesome, lonesome; yea,
E'en I, the brook, until this day.
Cast off your shoon; ah, come to me,
And I will love you lingeringly!

O wild brook, O wise brook, I cannot come, alas!
I am but mortal as the leaves that flicker, float, and pass.
My body is not used to you; my breath is fluttering sore;
You clasp me round too icily. Ah, let me go once more!
Would God I were a naiad-thing whereon Pan's music blew;
But woe is me! you pagan brook, I cannot stay with you!

Fannie Stearns Davis.

BACCHUS

LISTEN to the tawny thief,
Hid beneath the waxen leaf,
Growling at his fairy host,
Bidding her with angry boast
Fill his cup with wine distilled
From the dew the dawn has spilled:
Stored away in golden casks
Is the precious draught he asks.

Who, — who makes this mimic din
In this mimic meadow inn,
Sings in such a drowsy note,
Wears a golden-belted coat;
Loiters in the dainty room
Of this tavern of perfume;
Dares to linger at the cup
Till the yellow sun is up?

Bacchus 't is, come back again
To the busy haunts of men;
Garlanded and gaily dressed,
Bands of gold about his breast;
Straying from his paradise,
Having pinions angel-wise, —
'T is the honey-bee, who goes
Reveling within a rose!

Frank Dempster Sherman.

DA LEETLA BOY

DA spreeng ees com'! but oh, da joy
  Eet ees too late!
He was so cold, my leetla boy,
  He no could wait.

I no can count how manny week,
How manny day, dat he ees seeck;
How manny night I seet an' hold
Da leetla hand dat was so cold.
He was so patience, oh, so sweet!
Eet hurts my throat for theenk of eet;
An' all he evra ask ees w'en
Ees gona com' da spreeng agen.
Wan day, wan brighta sunny day,
He see, across da alleyway,
Da leetla girl dat's livin' dere
Ees raise her window for da air,
An' put outside a leetla pot
Of — w'at-you-call? — forgat-me-not.
So smalla flower, so leetla theeng!
But steell eet mak' hees hearta seeng:
"Oh, now, at las', ees com' da spreeng!
Da leetla plant ees glad for know
Da sun ees com' for mak' eet grow.
So, too, I am grow warm and strong."
So lika dat he seeng hees song.
But, Ah! da night com' down an' den
Da weenter ees sneak back agen,
An' een da alley all da night
Ees fall da snow, so cold, so white,
An' cover up da leetla pot

Of — wa't-you-call? — forgat-me-not.
All night da leetla hand I hold
Ees grow so cold, so cold, so cold!

Da spreeng ees com'; but oh, da joy
  Eet ees too late!
He was so cold, my leetla boy,
  He no could wait.

Thomas Augustine Daly.

AGAMEDE'S SONG

Grow, grow, thou little tree,
His body at the roots of thee;
Since last year's loveliness in death
The living beauty nourisheth.

Bloom, bloom, thou little tree,
Thy roots around the heart of me;
Thou canst not blow too white and fair
From all the sweetness hidden there.

Die, die, thou little tree,
And be as all sweet things must be;
Deep where thy petals drift I, too,
Would rest the changing seasons through.

Arthur Upson.

WHY

For a name unknown,
Whose fame unblown
Sleeps in the hills
    For ever and aye;

For her who hears
The stir of the years
Go by on the wind
    By night and day;

And heeds no thing
Of the needs of Spring,
Of Autumn's wonder
    Or Winter's chill;

For one who sees
The great sun freeze,
As he wanders a-cold
    From hill to hill;

And all her heart
Is a woven part
Of the flurry and drift
    Of whirling snow;

For the sake of two
Sad eyes and true,
And the old, old love
    So long ago.

Bliss Carman.

THE WIFE FROM FAIRYLAND

Her talk was all of woodland things,
  Of little lives that pass
Away in one green afternoon,
  Deep in the haunted grass;

For she had come from fairyland,
  The morning of a day
When the world that still was April
  Was turning into May.

Green leaves and silence and two eyes —
  'T was so she seemed to me,
A silver shadow of the woods,
  Whisper and mystery.

I looked into her woodland eyes,
  And all my heart was hers,
And then I led her by the hand
  Home up my marble stairs;

And all my granite and my gold
  Was hers for her green eyes,
And all my sinful heart was hers
  From sunset to sunrise;

I gave her all delight and ease
  That God had given to me,
I listened to fulfill her dreams,
  Rapt with expectancy.

But all I gave, and all I did,
  Brought but a weary smile
Of gratitude upon her face;
  As though a little while,

She loitered in magnificence
  Of marble and of gold,
And waited to be home again
  When the dull tale was told.

Sometimes, in the chill galleries,
  Unseen, she deemed, unheard,
I found her dancing like a leaf
  And singing like a bird.

So lone a thing I never saw
  In lonely earth or sky,
So merry and so sad a thing,
  One sad, one laughing, eye.

There came a day when on her heart
  A wildwood blossom lay,
And the world that still was April
  Was turning into May.

In the green eyes I saw a smile
  That turned my heart to stone:
My wife that came from fairyland
  No longer was alone.

For there had come a little hand
  To show the green way home,
Home through the leaves, home through the dew,
  Home through the greenwood — home.

Richard Le Gallienne.

LIFE

Life burns us up like fire,
  And Song goes up in flame:
The radiant body smoulders
  To the ashes whence it came.

Out of things it rises
  With a mouth that laughs and sings,
Backward it fades and falters
  Into the char of things.

Yet soars a voice above it —
  Love is holy and strong;
The best of us forever
  Escapes in Love and Song.

John Hall Wheelock.

SONG IS SO OLD

Song is so old,
Love is so new —
Let me be still
And kneel to you.

Let me be still
And breathe no word,
Save what my warm blood
Sings unheard.

Let my warm blood
Sing low of you —
Song is so fair,
Love is so new!

Hermann Hagedorn.

THAT DAY YOU CAME

Such special sweetness was about
  That day God sent you here,

I knew the lavender was out,
  And it was mid of year.

Their common way the great winds blew,
  The ships sailed out to sea;
Yet ere that day was spent I knew
  Mine own had come to me.

As after song some snatch of tune
  Lurks still in grass or bough,
So, somewhat of the end o' June
  Lurks in each weather now.

The young year sets the buds astir,
  The old year strips the trees;
But ever in my lavender
  I hear the brawling bees.

Lizette Woodworth Reese.

SONG

For me the jasmine buds unfold
  And silver daisies star the lea,
The crocus hoards the sunset gold,
  And the wild rose breathes for me.
I feel the sap through the bough returning,
  I share the skylark's transport fine,
I know the fountain's wayward yearning,
  I love, and the world is mine!

I love, and thoughts that sometime grieved,
  Still well remembered, grieve not me;

From all that darkened and deceived
  Upsoars my spirit free.
For soft the hours repeat one story,
  Sings the sea one strain divine;
My clouds arise all flushed with glory —
  I love, and the world is mine!

Florence Earle Coates.

MOTHER

I HAVE praised many loved ones in my song,
      And yet I stand
Before her shrine, to whom all things belong,
      With empty hand.

Perhaps the ripening future holds a time
      For things unsaid;
Not now; men do not celebrate in rhyme
      Their daily bread.

Theresa Helburn.

SONGS FOR MY MOTHER

I

HER HANDS

My mother's hands are cool and fair,
  They can do anything.
Delicate mercies hide them there
  Like flowers in the spring.

When I was small and could not sleep,
  She used to come to me,

And with my cheek upon her hand
  How sure my rest would be.

For everything she ever touched
  Of beautiful or fine,
Their memories living in her hands
  Would warm that sleep of mine.

Her hands remember how they played
  One time in meadow streams, —
And all the flickering song and shade
  Of water took my dreams.

Swift through her haunted fingers pass
  Memories of garden things; —
I dipped my face in flowers and grass
  And sounds of hidden wings.

One time she touched the cloud that kissed
  Brown pastures bleak and far; —
I leaned my cheek into a mist
  And thought I was a star.

All this was very long ago
  And I am grown; but yet
The hand that lured my slumber so
  I never can forget.

For still when drowsiness comes on
  It seems so soft and cool,
Shaped happily beneath my cheek,
  Hollow and beautiful.

II

HER WORDS

My mother has the prettiest tricks
  Of words and words and words.
Her talk comes out as smooth and sleek
  As breasts of singing birds.

She shapes her speech all silver fine
  Because she loves it so.
And her own eyes begin to shine
  To hear her stories grow.

And if she goes to make a call
  Or out to take a walk
We leave our work when she returns
  And run to hear her talk.

We had not dreamed these things were so
  Of sorrow and of mirth.
Her speech is as a thousand eyes
  Through which we see the earth.

God wove a web of loveliness,
  Of clouds and stars and birds,
But made not any thing at all
  So beautiful as words.

They shine around our simple earth
  With golden shadowings,
And every common thing they touch
  Is exquisite with wings.

There's nothing poor and nothing small
  But is made fair with them.
They are the hands of living faith
  That touch the garment's hem.

They are as fair as bloom or air,
  They shine like any star,
And I am rich who learned from her
  How beautiful they are.

Anna Hempstead Branch.

THE DAGUERREOTYPE

This, then, is she,
My mother as she looked at seventeen,
When she first met my father. Young incredibly,
Younger than spring, without the faintest trace
Of disappointment, weariness, or tean
Upon the childlike earnestness and grace
Of the waiting face.
Those close-wound ropes of pearl
(Or common beads made precious by their use)
Seem heavy for so slight a throat to wear;
But the low bodice leaves the shoulders bare
And half the glad swell of the breast, for news
That now the woman stirs within the girl.
And yet,
Even so, the loops and globes
Of beaten gold
And jet
Hung, in the stately way of old,
From the ears' drooping lobes

On festivals and Lord's-day of the week,
Show all too matron-sober for the cheek, —
Which, now I look again, is perfect child,
Or no — or no — 't is girlhood's very self,
Moulded by some deep, mischief-ridden elf
So meek, so maiden mild,
But startling the close gazer with the sense
Of passions forest-shy and forest-wild,
And delicate delirious merriments.

As a moth beats sidewise
And up and over, and tries
To skirt the irresistible lure
Of the flame that has him sure,
My spirit, that is none too strong to-day,
Flutters and makes delay, —
Pausing to wonder on the perfect lips,
Lifting to muse upon the low-drawn hair
And each hid radiance there,
But powerless to stem the tide-race bright,
The vehement peace which drifts it toward the light
Where soon — ah, now, with cries
Of grief and giving-up unto its gain
It shrinks no longer nor denies,
But dips
Hurriedly home to the exquisite heart of pain, —
And all is well, for I have seen them plain,
The unforgettable, the unforgotten eyes!
Across the blinding gush of these good tears
They shine as in the sweet and heavy years
When by her bed and chair
We children gathered jealously to share
The sunlit aura breathing myrrh and thyme,

Where the sore-stricken body made a clime
Gentler than May and pleasanter than rhyme,
Holier and more mystical than prayer.

God, how thy ways are strange!
That this should be, even this,
The patient head
Which suffered years ago the dreary change!
That these so dewy lips should be the same
As those I stooped to kiss
And heard my harrowing half-spoken name,
A little ere the one who bowed above her,
Our father and her very constant lover,
Rose stoical, and we knew that she was dead.
Then I, who could not understand or share
His antique nobleness,
Being unapt to bear
The insults which time flings us for our proof,
Fled from the horrible roof
Into the alien sunshine merciless,
The shrill satiric fields ghastly with day,
Raging to front God in his pride of sway
And hurl across the lifted swords of fate
That ringed Him where He sat
My puny gage of scorn and desolate hate
Which somehow should undo Him, after all!
That this girl face, expectant, virginal,
Which gazes out at me
Boon as a sweetheart, as if nothing loth
(Save for the eyes, with other presage stored)
To pledge me troth,
And in the kingdom where the heart is lord
Take sail on the terrible gladness of the deep

Whose winds the gray Norns keep, —
That this should be indeed
The flesh which caught my soul, a flying seed,
Out of the to and fro
Of scattering hands where the seedsman Mage,
Stooping from star to star and age to age
Sings as he sows!
That underneath this breast
Nine moons I fed
Deep of divine unrest,
While over and over in the dark she said,
"Blessèd! but not as happier children blessed" —
That this should be
Even she . . .
God, how with time and change
Thou makest thy footsteps strange!
Ah, now I know
They play upon me, and it is not so.
Why, 't is a girl I never saw before,
A little thing to flatter and make weep,
To tease until her heart is sore,
Then kiss and clear the score;
A gypsy run-the-fields,
A little liberal daughter of the earth,
Good for what hour of truancy and mirth
The careless season yields
Hither-side the flood of the year and yonder of the neap;
Then thank you, thanks again, and twenty light good-
byes. —
O shrined above the skies,
Frown not, clear brow,
Darken not, holy eyes!
Thou knowest well I know that it is thou

Only to save me from such memories
As would unman me quite,
Here in this web of strangeness caught
And prey to troubled thought
Do I devise
These foolish shifts and slight;
Only to shield me from the afflicting sense
Of some waste influence
Which from this morning face and lustrous hair
Breathes on me sudden ruin and despair.
In any other guise,
With any but this girlish depth of gaze,
Your coming had not so unsealed and poured
The dusty amphoras where I had stored
The drippings of the winepress of my days.
I think these eyes foresee,
Now in their unawakened virgin time,
Their mother's pride in me,
And dream even now, unconsciously,
Upon each soaring peak and sky-hung lea
You pictured I should climb.
Broken premonitions come,
Shapes, gestures visionary,
Not as once to maiden Mary
The manifest angel with fresh lilies came
Intelligibly calling her by name;
But vanishingly, dumb,
Thwarted and bright and wild,
As heralding a sin-defiled,
Earth-encumbered, blood-begotten, passionate man-child,
Who yet should be a trump of mighty call
Blown in the gates of evil kings

To make them fall;
Who yet should be a sword of flame before
The soul's inviolate door
To beat away the clang of hellish wings;
Who yet should be a lyre
Of high unquenchable desire
In the day of little things. —
Look, where the amphoras,
The yield of many days,
Trod by my hot soul from the pulp of self,
And set upon the shelf
In sullen pride
The Vineyard-master's tasting to abide —
O mother mine!
Are these the bringings-in, the doings fine,
Of him you used to praise?
Emptied and overthrown
The jars lie strown.
These, for their flavor duly nursed,
Drip from the stopples vinegar accursed;
These, I thought honied to the very seal,
Dry, dry, — a little acid meal,
A pinch of mouldy dust,
Sole leavings of the amber-mantling must;
These, rude to look upon,
But flasking up the liquor dearest won,
Through sacred hours and hard,
With watching and with wrestlings and with grief,
Even of these, of these in chief,
The stale breath sickens reeking from the shard.
Nothing is left. Aye, how much less than naught!
What shall be said or thought
Of the slack hours and waste imaginings,

The cynic rending of the wings,
Known to that froward, that unreckoning heart
Whereof this brewage was the precious part,
Treasured and set away with furtive boast?
O dear and cruel ghost,
Be merciful, be just!
See, I was yours and I am in the dust.
Then look not so, as if all things were well!
Take your eyes from me, leave me to my shame,
Or else, if gaze they must,
Steel them with judgment, darken them with blame;
But by the ways of light ineffable
You bade me go and I have faltered from,
By the low waters moaning out of hell
Whereto my feet have come,
Lay not on me these intolerable
Looks of rejoicing love, of pride, of happy trust!

Nothing dismayed?
By all I say and all I hint not made
Afraid?
O then, stay by me! Let
These eyes afflict me, cleanse me, keep me yet,
Brave eyes and true!
See how the shrivelled heart, that long has lain
Dead to delight and pain,
Stirs, and begins again
To utter pleasant life, as if it knew
The wintry days were through;
As if in its awakening boughs it heard
The quick, sweet-spoken bird.
Strong eyes and brave,
Inexorable to save!

William Vaughn Moody.

TEARS

When I consider Life and its few years —
A wisp of fog betwixt us and the sun;
A call to battle, and the battle done
Ere the last echo dies within our ears;
A rose choked in the grass; an hour of fears;
The gusts that past a darkening shore do beat;
The burst of music down an unlistening street, —
I wonder at the idleness of tears.
Ye old, old dead, and ye of yesternight,
Chieftains, and bards, and keepers of the sheep,
By every cup of sorrow that you had,
Loose me from tears, and make me see aright
How each hath back what once he stayed to weep:
Homer his sight, David his little lad!

Lizette Woodworth Reese.

THE SEA-LANDS

Would I were on the sea-lands,
  Where winds know how to sting;
And in the rocks at midnight
  The lost long murmurs sing.

Would I were with my first love
  To hear the rush and roar
Of spume below the doorstep
  And winds upon the door.

My first love was a fair girl
  With ways forever new;

And hair a sunlight yellow,
  And eyes a morning blue.

The roses, have they tarried
  Or are they dun and frayed?
If we had stayed together,
  Would love, indeed, have stayed?

Ah, years are filled with learning,
  And days are leaves of change!
And I have met so many
  I knew . . . and found them strange.

But on the sea-lands tumbled
  By winds that sting and blind,
The nights we watched, so silent,
  Come back, come back to mind. .

I mind about my first love,
  And hear the rush and roar
Of spume below the doorstep
  And winds upon the door.

Orrick Johns.

BAG-PIPES AT SEA

Above the shouting of the gale,
  The whipping sheet, the dashing spray,
I heard, with notes of joy and wail,
A piper play.

Along the dipping deck he trod,
  The dusk about his shadowy form;

He seemed like some strange ancient god
  Of song and storm.

He gave his dim-seen pipes a skirl
  And war went down the darkling air;
Then came a sudden subtle swirl,
  And love was there.

What were the winds that flailed and flayed
  The sea to him, the night obscure?
In dreams he strayed some brackened glade,
  Some heathery moor.

And if he saw the slanting spars,
  And if he watched the shifting track,
He marked, too, the eternal stars
  Shine through the wrack.

And so amid the deep sea din,
  And so amid the wastes of foam,
Afar his heart was happy in
  His highland home!

Clinton Scollard.

THE HEART'S COUNTRY

Hill people turn to their hills;
  Sea-folk are sick for the sea:
Thou art my land and my country,
  And my heart calls out for thee.

The bird beats his wings for the open,
  The captive burns to be free;

But I — I cry at thy window,
  For thou art my liberty.
Florence Wilkinson.

JOYOUS-GARD

WIND-WASHED and free, full-swept by rain and wave,
  By tang of surf and thunder of the gale,
  Wild be the ride yet safe the barque will sail
And past the plunging seas her harbor brave;
Nor care have I that storms and waters rave,
  I cannot fear since you can never fail —
  Once have I looked upon the burning grail,
And through your eyes have seen beyond the grave.

I know at last — the strange, sweet mystery,
  The nameless joy that trembled into tears,
    The hush of wings when you were at my side —
For now the veil is rent and I can see,
  See the true vision of the future years,
    As in your face the love of Him who died!
Thomas S. Jones, Jr.

THE SECRET

NIGHTINGALES warble about it,
  All night under blossom and star;
The wild swan is dying without it,
  And the eagle crieth afar;
The sun he doth mount but to find it,
  Searching the green earth o'er;
But more doth a man's heart mind it,
  Oh, more, more, more!

Over the gray leagues of ocean
  The infinite yearneth alone;
The forests with wandering emotion
  The thing they know not intone;
Creation arose but to see it,
  A million lamps in the blue;
But a lover he shall be it
  If one sweet maid is true.

George Edward Woodberry.

THE NIGHTINGALE UNHEARD

Yes, Nightingale, through all the summer-time
  We followed on, from moon to golden moon;
  From where Salerno day-dreams in the noon,
And the far rose of Pæstum once did climb.
  All the white way beside the girdling blue,
Through sun-shrill vines and campanile chime,
  We listened; — from the old year to the new.
    Brown bird, and where were you?

You, that Ravello lured not, throned on high
  And filled with singing out of sun-burned throats!
  Nor yet Minore of the flame-sailed boats;
Nor yet — of all bird-song should glorify —
  Assisi, Little Portion of the blest,
Assisi, in the bosom of the sky,
  Where God's own singer thatched his sunward nest;
    That little, heavenliest!

And north and north, to where the hedge-rows are,
  That beckon with white looks an endless way;

Where, through the fair wet silverness of May,
A lamb shines out as sudden as a star,
Among the cloudy sheep; and green, and pale,
The may-trees reach and glimmer, near or far,
And the red may-trees wear a shining veil.
And still, no nightingale!

The one vain longing, — through all journeyings,
The one: in every hushed and hearkening spot, —
All the soft-swarming dark where you were not,
Still longed for! Yes, for sake of dreams and wings,
And wonders, that your own must ever make
To bower you close, with all hearts' treasurings;
And for that speech toward which all hearts do ache; —
Even for Music's sake.

But most, his music whose belovèd name
Forever writ in water of bright tears,
Wins to one grave-side even the Roman years,
That kindle there the hallowed April flame
Of comfort-breathing violets. By that shrine
Of Youth, Love, Death, forevermore the same,
Violets still! — When falls, to leave no sign,
The arch of Constantine.

Most for his sake we dreamed. Tho' not as he,
From that lone spirit, brimmed with human woe,
Your song once shook to surging overflow.
How was it, sovran dweller of the tree,
His cry, still throbbing in the flooded shell
Of silence with remembered melody,
Could draw from you no answer to the spell?
— O Voice, O Philomel?

Long time we wondered (and we knew not why): —
  Nor dream, nor prayer, of wayside gladness born,
  Nor vineyards waiting, nor reproachful thorn,
Nor yet the nested hill-towns set so high
  All the white way beside the girdling blue, —
Nor olives, gray against a golden sky,
  Could serve to wake that rapturous voice of you!
    But the wise silence knew.

O Nightingale unheard! — Unheard alone,
  Throughout that woven music of the days
  From the faint sea-rim to the market-place,
And ring of hammers on cathedral stone!
  So be it, better so: that there should fail
For sun-filled ones, one blessèd thing unknown.
  To them, be hid forever, — and all hail!
    Sing never, Nightingale.

Sing, for the others! Sing; to some pale cheek
  Against the window, like a starving flower.
  Loose, with your singing, one poor pilgrim hour
Of journey, with some Heart's Desire to seek.
  Loose, with your singing, captives such as these
In misery and iron, hearts too meek,
  For voyage — voyage over dreamful seas
    To lost Hesperides.

Sing not for free-men. Ah, but sing for whom
  The walls shut in; and even as eyes that fade,
  The windows take no heed of light nor shade, —
The leaves are lost in mutterings of the loom.
  Sing near! So in that golden overflowing
They may forget their wasted human bloom;

Pay the devouring days their all, unknowing, —
Reck not of life's bright going!

Sing not for lovers, side by side that hark;
Nor unto parted lovers, save they be
Parted indeed by more than makes the Sea,
Where never hope shall meet — like mounting lark —
Far Joy's uprising; and no memories
Abide to star the music-haunted dark:
To them that sit in darkness, such as these,
Pour down, pour down heart's-ease.

Not in Kings' gardens. No; but where there haunt
The world's forgotten, both of men and birds;
The alleys of no hope and of no words,
The hidings where men reap not, though they plant;
But toil and thirst — so dying and so born; —
And toil and thirst to gather to their want,
From the lean waste, beyond the daylight's scorn,
— To gather grapes of thorn!

. . . .

And for those two, your pilgrims without tears,
Who prayed a largess where there was no dearth,
Forgive it to their human-happy ears:
Forgive it them, brown music of the Earth,
Unknowing, — though the wiser silence knew!
Forgive it to the music of the spheres
That while they walked together so, the Two
Together, — heard not you.

Josephine Preston Peabody.

ONLY OF THEE AND ME

Only of thee and me the night wind sings,
Only of us the sailors speak at sea,
The earth is filled with wondered whisperings
Only of thee and me.

Only of thee and me the breakers chant,
Only of us the stir in bush and tree;
The rain and sunshine tell the eager plant
Only of thee and me.

Only of thee and me, till all shall fade;
Only of us the whole world's thoughts can be —
For we are Love, and God Himself is made
Only of thee and me.

Louis Untermeyer.

WHEN THE WIND IS LOW

When the wind is low, and the sea is soft,
And the far heat-lightning plays
On the rim of the west where dark clouds nest
On a darker bank of haze;
When I lean o'er the rail with you that I love
And gaze to my heart's content;
I know that the heavens are there above —
But you are my firmament.

When the phosphor-stars are thrown from the bow
And the watch climbs up the shroud;
When the dim mast dips as the vessel slips
Through the foam that seethes aloud;

I know that the years of our life are few,
  And fain as a bird to flee,
That time is as brief as a drop of dew —
  But you are Eternity.

Cale Young Rice.

LOVE TRIUMPHANT

Helen's lips are drifting dust;
Ilion is consumed with rust;
All the galleons of Greece
Drink the ocean's dreamless peace;
Lost was Solomon's purple show
Restless centuries ago;
Stately empires wax and wane —
Babylon, Barbary, and Spain; —
Only one thing, undefaced,
Lasts, though all the worlds lie waste
And the heavens are overturned.
Dear, how long ago we learned!

There's a sight that blinds the sun,
Sound that lives when sounds are done,
Music that rebukes the birds,
Language lovelier than words,
Hue and scent that shame the rose,
Wine no earthly vineyard knows,
Silence stiller than the shore
Swept by Charon's stealthy oar,
Ocean more divinely free
Than Pacific's boundless sea, —
Ye who love have learned it true.
Dear, how long ago we knew!

Frederic Lawrence Knowles.

BE STILL. THE HANGING GARDENS WERE A DREAM

Be still. The Hanging Gardens were a dream
That over Persian roses flew to kiss
The curlèd lashes of Semiramis.
Troy never was, nor green Skamander stream.
Provence and Troubadour are merest lies,
The glorious hair of Venice was a beam
Made within Titian's eye. The sunsets seem,
The world is very old and nothing is.
Be still. Thou foolish thing, thou canst not wake,
Nor thy tears wedge thy soldered lids apart,
But patter in the darkness of thy heart.
Thy brain is plagued. Thou art a frighted owl
Blind with the light of life thou'ldst not forsake,
And Error loves and nourishes thy soul.

Trumbull Stickney.

THE TEARS OF HARLEQUIN

To you he gave his laughter and his jest,
His words that of all words were merriest,
His glad, mad moments when the lights flared high
And his wild song outshrilled the plaudits' din.
For you that memory, but happier I —
I, who have known the tears of Harlequin.

Not mine those moments when the roses lay
Like red spilled wine on his triumphant way,
And shouts acclaimed him through the music's beat,
Above the voice of flute and violin.
But I have known his hour of sore defeat —
I — I have known the tears of Harlequin.

Light kisses and light words, they were not mine —
Poor perquisites of many a Columbine
  Bought with his laughter, flattered by his jest;
But when despair broke through the painted grin,
  His tortured face has fallen on my breast —
I — I have known the tears of Harlequin.

You weep for him, who look upon him dead,
That joy and jest and merriment are fled;
  You weep for him, what time my eyes are dry,
Knowing what peace a weary soul may win
  Stifled by too much masking — even I —
I, who have known the tears of Harlequin.

Theodosia Garrison.

THE BURIED CITY

My heart is like a city of the gay
  Reared on the ruins of a perished one
  Wherein my dead loves cower from the sun,
White-swathed like kings, the Pharaohs of a day.
Within the buried city stirs no sound,
  Save for the bat, forgetful of the rod,
  Perched on the knee of some deserted god,
And for the groan of rivers underground.

Stray not, my Love, 'mid the sarcophagi —
  Tempt not the silence, for the fates are deep,
Lest all the dreamers, deeming doomsday nigh,
  Leap forth in terror from their haunted sleep;
And like the peal of an accursèd bell
Thy voice call ghosts of dead things back from hell.

George Sylvester Viereck.

THE RIDE TO THE LADY

"Now since mine even is come at last, —
For I have been the sport of steel,
And hot life ebbeth from me fast,
And I in saddle roll and reel, —
Come bind me, bind me on my steed!
Of fingering leech I have no need!"
The chaplain clasped his mailèd knee.
"Nor need I more thy whine and thee!
No time is left my sins to tell;
But look ye bind me, bind me well!"
They bound him strong with leathern thong,
For the ride to the lady should be long.

Day was dying; the poplars fled,
Thin as ghosts, on a sky blood-red;
Out of the sky the fierce hue fell,
And made the streams as the streams of hell.
All his thoughts as a river flowed,
Flowed aflame as fleet he rode,
Onward flowed to her abode,
Ceased at her feet, mirrored her face.
(Viewless Death apace, apace,
Rode behind him in that race.)

'Face, mine own, mine alone,
Trembling lips my lips have known,
Birdlike stir of the dove-soft eyne
Under the kisses that make them mine!
Only of thee, of thee, my need!
Only to thee, to thee, I speed!"
The Cross flashed by at the highway's turn;
In a beam of the moon the Face shone stern.

Far behind had the fight's din died;
The shuddering stars in the welkin wide
Crowded, crowded, to see him ride.
The beating hearts of the stars aloof
Kept time to the beat of the horse's hoof.
"What is the throb that thrills so sweet?
Heart of my lady, I feel it beat!"
But his own strong pulse the fainter fell,
Like the failing tongue of a hushing bell.
The flank of the great-limbed steed was wet
Not alone with the started sweat.

Fast, and fast, and the thick black wood
Arched its cowl like a black friar's hood;
Fast, and fast, and they plunged therein, —
But the viewless rider rode to win.

Out of the wood to the highway's light
Galloped the great-limbed steed in fright;
The mail clashed cold, and the sad owl cried,
And the weight of the dead oppressed his side.

Fast, and fast, by the road he knew;
And slow, and slow, the stars withdrew;
And the waiting heaven turned weirdly blue,
As a garment worn of a wizard grim.
He neighed at the gate in the morning dim.

She heard no sound before her gate,
Though very quiet was her bower.
All was as her hand had left it late:
The needle slept on the broidered vine,
Where the hammer and spikes of the passion-flower
Her fashioning did wait.

On the couch lay something fair,
With steadfast lips and veilèd eyne;
But the lady was not there.
On the wings of shrift and prayer,
Pure as winds that winnow snow,
Her soul had risen twelve hours ago.
The burdened steed at the barred gate stood,
No whit the nearer to his goal.
Now God's great grace assoil the soul
That went out in the wood!

Helen Gray Cone.

EVENSONG

Beauty calls and gives no warning,
Shadows rise and wander on the day.
In the twilight, in the quiet evening,
We shall rise and smile and go away.
Over the flaming leaves
Freezes the sky.
It is the season grieves,
Not you, not I.
All our spring-times, all our summers,
We have kept the longing warm within.
Now we leave the after-comers
To attain the dreams we did not win.
O we have wakened, Sweet, and had our birth,
And that's the end of earth;
And we have toiled and smiled and kept the light,
And that's the end of night.

Ridgely Torrence.

WITCHERY

OUT of the purple drifts,
  From the shadow sea of night,
On tides of musk a moth uplifts
  Its weary wings of white.

Is it a dream or ghost
  Of a dream that comes to me,
Here in the twilight on the coast,
  Blue cinctured by the sea?

Fashioned of foam and froth —
  And the dream is ended soon,
And lo, whence came the moon-white moth
  Comes now the moth-white moon!

Frank Dempster Sherman.

GOLDEN PULSE

GOLDEN pulse grew on the shore,
  Ferns along the hill,
And the red cliff roses bore
  Bees to drink their fill;

Bees that from the meadows bring
  Wine of melilot,
Honey-sups on golden wing
  To the garden grot.

But to me, neglected flower,
  Phaon will not see,

Passion brings no crowning hour,
Honey nor the bee.

John Myers O'Hara.

SAPPHO

THE twilight's inner flame grows blue and deep,
And in my Lesbos, over leagues of sea,
The temples glimmer moonwise in the trees.
Twilight has veiled the little flower face
Here on my heart, but still the night is kind
And leaves her warm sweet weight against my breast.
Am I that Sappho who would run at dusk
Along the surges creeping up the shore
When tides came in to ease the hungry beach,
And running, running, till the night was black,
Would fall forespent upon the chilly sand
And quiver with the winds from off the sea?
Ah, quietly the shingle waits the tides
Whose waves are stinging kisses, but to me
Love brought no peace, nor darkness any rest.
I crept and touched the foam with fevered hands
And cried to Love, from whom the sea is sweet,
From whom the sea is bitterer than death.
Ah, Aphrodite, if I sing no more
To thee, God's daughter, powerful as God,
It is that thou hast made my life too sweet
To hold the added sweetness of a song.
There is a quiet at the heart of love,
And I have pierced the pain and come to peace.
I hold my peace, my Cleïs, on my heart;
And softer than a little wild bird's wing

Are kisses that she pours upon my mouth.
Ah, never any more when spring like fire
Will flicker in the newly opened leaves,
Shall I steal forth to seek for solitude
Beyond the lure of light Alcæus' lyre,
Beyond the sob that stilled Erinna's voice.
Ah, never with a throat that aches with song,
Beneath the white uncaring sky of spring,
Shall I go forth to hide awhile from Love
The quiver and the crying of my heart.
Still I remember how I strove to flee
The love-note of the birds, and bowed my head
To hurry faster, but upon the ground
I saw two wingèd shadows side by side,
And all the world's spring passion stifled me.
Ah, Love, there is no fleeing from thy might,
No lonely place where thou hast never trod,
No desert thou hast left uncarpeted
With flowers that spring beneath thy perfect feet.
In many guises didst thou come to me;
I saw thee by the maidens while they danced,
Phaon allured me with a look of thine,
In Anactoria I knew thy grace,
I looked at Cercolas and saw thine eyes;
But never wholly, soul and body mine,
Didst thou bid any love me as I loved.
Now I have found the peace that fled from me;
Close, close, against my heart I hold my world.
Ah, Love that made my life a lyric cry,
Ah, Love that tuned my lips to lyres of thine,
I taught the world thy music, now alone
I sing for one who falls asleep to hear.

Sara Teasdale.

HARPS HUNG UP IN BABYLON

THE harps hung up in Babylon,
Their loosened strings rang on, sang on,
And cast their murmurs forth upon
The roll and roar of Babylon:
"*Forget me, Lord, if I forget*
Jerusalem for Babylon,
If I forget the vision set
High as the head of Lebanon
Is lifted over Syria yet,
If I forget and bow me down
To brutish gods of Babylon."

Two rivers to each other run
In the very midst of Babylon,
And swifter than their current fleets
The restless river of the streets
Of Babylon, of Babylon,
And Babylon's towers smite the sky,
But higher reeks to God most high
The smoke of her iniquity:
"*But oh, betwixt the green and blue*
To walk the hills that once we knew
When you were pure and I was true," —
So rang the harps in Babylon —
"*Or ere along the roads of stone*
Had led us captive one by one
The subtle gods of Babylon."

The harps hung up in Babylon
Hung silent till the prophet dawn,
When Judah's feet the highway burned
Back to the holy hills returned,

And shook their dust on Babylon.
In Zion's halls the wild harps rang,
To Zion's walls their smitten clang,
And lo! of Babylon they sang,
They only sang of Babylon:
"*Jehovah, round whose throne of awe*
The vassal stars their orbits draw
Within the circle of Thy law,
Canst thou make nothing what is done,
Or cause Thy servant to be one
That has not been in Babylon,
That has not known the power and pain
Of life poured out like driven rain?
I will go down and find again
My soul that 's lost in Babylon."

Arthur Colton.

LIVE BLINDLY

LIVE blindly and upon the hour. The Lord,
Who was the Future, died full long ago.
Knowledge which is the Past is folly. Go,
Poor child, and be not to thyself abhorred.
Around thine earth sun-wingèd winds do blow
And planets roll; a meteor draws his sword;
The rainbow breaks his seven-coloured chord
And the long strips of river-silver flow:
Awake! Give thyself to the lovely hours.
Drinking their lips, catch thou the dream in flight
About their fragile hairs' aërial gold.
Thou art divine, thou livest, — as of old
Apollo springing naked to the light,
And all his island shivered into flowers.

Trumbull Stickney.

LOVE'S SPRINGTIDE

My heart was winter-bound until
  I heard you sing;
O voice of Love, hush not, but fill
  My life with Spring!

My hopes were homeless things before
  I saw your eyes;
O smile of Love, close not the door
  To paradise!

My dreams were bitter once, and then
  I found them bliss;
O lips of Love, give me again
  Your rose to kiss!

Springtide of Love! The secret sweet
  Is ours alone;
O heart of Love, at last you beat
  Against my own!

Frank Dempster Sherman.

WANDERERS

Sweet is the highroad when the skylarks call,
  When we and Love go rambling through the land.
  But shall we still walk gayly, hand in hand,
At the road's turning and the twilight's fall?
Then darkness shall divide us like a wall,
  And uncouth evil nightbirds flap their wings;
  The solitude of all created things
Will creep upon us shuddering like a pall.

This is the knowledge I have wrung from pain:
We, yea, all lovers, are not one, but twain,
  Each by strange wisps to strange abysses drawn;
But through the black immensity of night
Love's little lantern, like a glowworm's, bright,
  May lead our steps to some stupendous dawn.

George Sylvester Viereck.

BALLADE OF MY LADY'S BEAUTY

SQUIRE ADAM had two wives, they say,
  Two wives had he, for his delight,
He kissed and clypt them all the day
  And clypt and kissed them all the night.
  Now Eve like ocean foam was white
And Lilith roses dipped in wine,
  But though they were a goodly sight
No lady is so fair as mine.

To Venus some folk tribute pay
  And Queen of Beauty she is hight,
And Sainte Marie the world doth sway
  In cerule napery bedight.
  My wonderment these twain invite,
Their comeliness it is divine,
  And yet I say in their despite,
No lady is so fair as mine.

Dame Helen caused a grievous fray,
  For love of her brave men did fight,
The eyes of her made sages fey
  And put their hearts in woeful plight.

To her no rhymes will I indite,
For her no garlands will I twine,
Though she be made of flowers and light
No lady is so fair as mine.

L'ENVOI

Prince Eros, Lord of lovely might,
Who on Olympus dost recline,
Do I not tell the truth aright?
No lady is so fair as mine.

Joyce Kilmer.

GRIEVE NOT, LADIES

Oh, grieve not, Ladies, if at night
Ye wake to feel your beauty going.
It was a web of frail delight,
Inconstant as an April snowing.

In other eyes, in other lands,
In deep fair pools, new beauty lingers,
But like spent water in your hands
It runs from your reluctant fingers.

Ye shall not keep the singing lark
That owes to earlier skies its duty.
Weep not to hear along the dark
The sound of your departing beauty.

The fine and anguished ear of night
Is tuned to hear the smallest sorrow.
Oh, wait until the morning light!
It may not seem so gone to-morrow!

But honey-pale and rosy-red!
  Brief lights that made a little shining!
Beautiful looks about us shed —
  They leave us to the old repining.

Think not the watchful dim despair
  Has come to you the first, sweet-hearted!
For oh, the gold in Helen's hair!
  And how she cried when that departed!

Perhaps that one that took the most,
  The swiftest borrower, wildest spender,
May count, as we would not, the cost —
  And grow more true to us and tender.

Happy are we if in his eyes
  We see no shadow of forgetting.
Nay — if our star sinks in those skies
  We shall not wholly see its setting.

Then let us laugh as do the brooks
  That such immortal youth is ours,
If memory keeps for them our looks
  As fresh as are the spring-time flowers.

Oh, grieve not, Ladies, if at night
  Ye wake, to feel the cold December!
Rather recall the early light
  And in your loved one's arms, remember.

Anna Hempstead Branch.

OF JOAN'S YOUTH

I WOULD unto my fair restore
A simple thing:
The flushing cheek she had before!
Out-velveting
No more, no more,
On our sad shore,
The carmine grape, the moth's auroral wing.

Ah, say how winds in flooding grass
Unmoor the rose;
Or guileful ways the salmon pass
To sea, disclose:
For so, alas,
With Love, alas,
With fatal, fatal Love a girlhood goes.

Louise Imogen Guiney.

I SHALL NOT CARE

WHEN I am dead and over me bright April
  Shakes out her rain-drenched hair,
Though you should lean above me broken-hearted,
  I shall not care.

I shall have peace as leafy trees are peaceful,
  When rain bends down the bough,
And I shall be more silent and cold-hearted
  Than you are now.

Sara Teasdale.

LOVE CAME BACK AT FALL O' DEW

Love came back at fall o' dew,
Playing his old part;
But I had a word or two
That would break his heart.

"He who comes at candlelight,
That should come before,
Must betake him to the night
From a barrèd door."

This the word that made us part
In the fall o' dew;
This the word that brake his heart —
Yet it brake mine, too.

Lizette Woodworth Reese.

THERE'S ROSEMARY

O love that is not Love, but dear, so dear!
That is not love because it goes full soon,
Like flower born and dead within one moon,
And yet is love, for that it comes too near
The guarded fane where love alone may peer,
Ere, like young spring by summer soon outshone,
It trembles into death; yet comes anon
As thoughts of spring will come though summer's here.

O star prelusive to a dream more fair,
Within my heart I'll keep a heaven for thee

Where thou mayst freely come and freely go,
Touching with thy faint gold ere I am 'ware
A twilight hope — a dawn I did not see —
O love that is not Love, but nearly so!

Olive Tilford Dargan.

LOVE'S RITUAL

Breathe me the ancient words when I shall find
Your spirit mine; if, seeking you, life wins
New wonder, with old splendor let us bind
Our hearts when Love's high sacrament begins.

Exalt my soul with pomp and pageantry,
Sing the eternal songs all lovers sing;
Yea, when you come, gold let our vestments be,
And lamps of silver let us softly swing.

But if at last, (hark how I whisper, Love!)
You from my temple and from me should turn,
I pray you chant no psalm my grief above,
Over the body of Pain let no light burn.

Go forth in silence, quiet as a dove,
Drift, with no sign, from our exultant place;
We need no *Ite* at the death of Love,
And none should come to look on Love's white face.

Charles Hanson Towne.

GREY ROCKS AND GREYER SEA

Grey rocks, and greyer sea,
And surf along the shore —

And in my heart a name
  My lips shall speak no more.

The high and lonely hills
  Endure the darkening year —
And in my heart endure
  A memory and a tear.

Across the tide a sail
  That tosses, and is gone —
And in my heart the kiss
  That longing dreams upon.

Grey rocks, and greyer sea,
  And surf along the shore —
And in my heart the face
  That I shall see no more.

Charles G. D. Roberts.

"GRANDMITHER, THINK NOT I FORGET"

Grandmither, think not I forget, when I come back to town,
An' wander the old ways again, an' tread them up and down.
I never smell the clover bloom, nor see the swallows pass,
Wi'out I mind how good ye were unto a little lass;
I never hear the winter rain a-pelting all night through
Wi'out I think and mind me of how cold it falls on you.
An' if I come not often to your bed beneath the thyme,
Mayhap 't is that I'd change wi' ye, and gie my bed for thine,
  Would like to sleep in thine.

I never hear the summer winds among the roses blow
Wi'out I wonder why it was ye loved the lassie so.
Ye gave me cakes and lollipops and pretty toys a score —
I never thought I should come back and ask ye now for more.
Grandmither, gie me your still white hands that lie upon your breast,
For mine do beat the dark all night and never find me rest;
They grope among the shadows an' they beat the cold black air,
They go seekin' in the darkness, an' they never find him there,
They never find him there.

Grandmither, gie me your sightless eyes, that I may never see
His own a-burnin' full o' love that must not shine for me.
Grandmither, gie me your peaceful lips, white as the kirkyard snow,
For mine be tremblin' wi' the wish that he must never know.
Grandmither, gie me your clay-stopped ears, that I may never hear
My lad a-singin' in the night when I am sick wi' fear;
A-singin' when the moonlight over a' the land is white —
Ah, God! I'll up and go to him, a-singin' in the night,
A-callin' in the night.

Grandmither, gie me your clay-cold heart, that has
forgot to ache,
For mine be fire wi'in my breast an' yet it cannot
break.
Wi' every beat it's callin' for things that must not
be, —
So can ye not let me creep in an' rest awhile by ye?
A little lass afeard o' dark slept by ye years agone —
An' she has found what night can hold 'twixt sunset
an' the dawn:
So when I plant the rose an' rue above your grave for
ye,
Ye'll know it's under rue an' rose that I would like to
be,
That I would like to be.

Willa Sibert Cather.

"WHEN I AM DEAD AND SISTER TO THE DUST"

When I am dead and sister to the dust;
When no more avidly I drink the wine
Of human love; when the pale Proserpine
Has covered me with poppies, and cold rust
Has cut my lyre-strings, and the sun has thrust
Me underground to nourish the world-vine, —
Men shall discover these old songs of mine,
And say: This woman lived — as poets must!

This woman lived and wore life as a sword
To conquer wisdom; this dead woman read
In the sealed Book of Love and underscored

The meanings. Then the sails of faith she spread,
And faring out for regions unexplored,
Went singing down the River of the Dead.

Elsa Barker.

LITTLE GRAY SONGS FROM ST. JOSEPH'S

I

WITH cassock black, baret and book,
Father Saran goes by;
I think he goes to say a prayer
For one who has to die.

Even so, some day, Father Saran
May say a prayer for me;
Myself meanwhile, the Sister tells,
Should pray unceasingly.

They kneel who pray: how may I kneel
Who face to ceiling lie,
Shut out by all that man has made
From God who made the sky?

They lift who pray — the low earth-born —
A humble heart to God:
But O, my heart of clay is proud —
True sister to the sod.

I look into the face of God,
They say bends over me;
I search the dark, dark face of God —
O what is it I see?

I see — who lie fast bound, who may
  Not kneel, who can but seek —
I see mine own face over me,
  With tears upon its cheek.

II

If my dark grandam had but known,
  Or yet my wild grandsir,
Or the lord that lured the maid away
  That was my sad mother,

O had they known, O had they dreamed
  What gift it was they gave,
Would they have stayed their wild, wild love,
  Nor made my years their slave?

Must they have stopped their hungry lips
  From love at thought of me?
O life, O life, how may we learn
  Thy strangest mystery?

Nay, they knew not, as we scarce know;
  Their souls, O let them rest;
My life is pupil unto pain —
  With him I make my quest.

III

My little soul I never saw,
  Nor can I count its days;
I do not know its wondrous law
  And yet I know its ways.

O it is young as morning-hours,
  And old as is the night;

O it has growth of budding flowers,
  Yet tastes my body's blight.

And it is silent and apart,
  And far and fair and still,
Yet ever beats within my heart,
  And cries within my will.

And it is light and bright and strange,
  And sees life far away,
Yet far with near can interchange
  And dwell within the day.

My soul has died a thousand deaths,
  And yet it does not die;
My soul has broke a thousand faiths,
  And yet it cannot lie;

My soul — there's naught can make it less;
  My soul — there's naught can mar;
Yet here it weeps with loneliness
  Within its lonely star.

My soul — not any dark can bind,
  Nor hinder any hand,
Yet here it weeps — long blind, long blind —
  And cannot understand.

Grace Fallow Norton.

IRISH PEASANT SONG

I TRY to knead and spin, but my life is low the while.
Oh, I long to be alone, and walk abroad a mile;

Yet if I walk alone, and think of naught at all,
Why from me that's young should the wild tears fall?

The shower-sodden earth, the earth-colored streams,
They breathe on me awake, and moan to me in
dreams,
And yonder ivy fondling the broke castle-wall,
It pulls upon my heart till the wild tears fall.

The cabin-door looks down a furze-lighted hill,
And far as Leighlin Cross the fields are green and still;
But once I hear the blackbird in Leighlin hedges call,
The foolishness is on me, and the wild tears fall!

Louise Imogen Guiney.

THE PRINCE

My heart it was a cup of gold
That at his lip did long to lie,
But he hath drunk the red wine down,
And tossed the goblet by.

My heart it was a floating bird
That through the world did wander free,
But he hath locked it in a cage,
And lost the silver key.

My heart it was a white, white rose
That bloomed upon a broken bough,
He did but wear it for an hour,
And it is withered now.

Josephine Dodge Daskam.

FOUR WINDS

"Four winds blowing thro' the sky,
You have seen poor maidens die,
Tell me then what I shall do
That my lover may be true."
Said the wind from out the south,
"Lay no kiss upon his mouth,"
And the wind from out the west,
"Wound the heart within his breast,"
And the wind from out the east,
"Send him empty from the feast,"
And the wind from out the north,
"In the tempest thrust him forth;
When thou art more cruel than he,
Then will Love be kind to thee."

Sara Teasdale.

A WEST-COUNTRY LOVER

Then, lady, at last thou art sick of my sighing.
Good-bye!
So long as I sue, thou wilt still be denying?
Good-bye!
Ah, well! shall I vow then to serve thee forever,
And swear no unkindness our kinship can sever?
Nay, nay, dear my lass! here's an end of endeavor.
Good-bye!

Yet let no sweet ruth for my misery grieve thee.
Good-bye!
The man who has loved knows as well how to leave thee.
Good-bye!

The gorse is enkindled, there's bloom on the heather,
And love is my joy, but so too is fair weather;
I still ride abroad though we ride not together.
Good-bye!

My horse is my mate; let the wind be my master.
Good-bye!
Though Care may pursue, yet my hound follows faster.
Good-bye!
The red deer's a-tremble in coverts unbroken.
He hears the hoof-thunder; he scents the death-token.
Shall I mope at home, under vows never spoken?
Good-bye!

The brown earth's my book, and I ride forth to read it.
Good-bye!
The stream runneth fast, but my will shall outspeed it.
Good-bye!
I love thee, dear lass, but I hate the hag Sorrow.
As sun follows rain, and to-night has its morrow,
So I'll taste of joy, though I steal, beg, or borrow!
Good-bye!

Alice Brown.

A WINTER RIDE

WHO shall declare the joy of the running!
Who shall tell of the pleasures of flight!
Springing and spurning the tufts of wild heather,
Sweeping, wide-winged, through the blue dome of light.
Everything mortal has moments immortal,
Swift and God-gifted, immeasurably bright.

So with the stretch of the white road before me,
  Shining snow crystals rainbowed by the sun,
Fields that are white, stained with long, cool, blue
    shadows,
  Strong with the strength of my horse as we run.
Joy in the touch of the wind and the sunlight!
  Joy! With the vigorous earth I am one.

Amy Lowell.

SIC VITA

Heart free, hand free,
  Blue above, brown under,
All the world to me
  Is a place of wonder.
Sun shine, moon shine,
  Stars, and winds a-blowing,
All into this heart of mine
  Flowing, flowing, flowing!

Mind free, step free,
  Days to follow after,
Joys of life sold to me
  For the price of laughter.
Girl's love, man's love,
  Love of work and duty,
Just a will of God's to prove
  Beauty, beauty, beauty!

William Stanley Braithwaite.

ACROSS THE FIELDS TO ANNE

How often in the summer-tide,
His graver business set aside,

Has stripling Will, the thoughtful-eyed,
As to the pipe of Pan,
Stepped blithesomely with lover's pride
Across the fields to Anne.

It must have been a merry mile,
This summer stroll by hedge and stile,
With sweet foreknowledge all the while
How sure the pathway ran
To dear delights of kiss and smile,
Across the fields to Anne.

The silly sheep that graze to-day,
I wot, they let him go his way,
Nor once looked up, as who should say:
"It is a seemly man."
For many lads went wooing aye
Across the fields to Anne.

The oaks, they have a wiser look;
Mayhap they whispered to the brook:
"The world by him shall yet be shook,
It is in nature's plan;
Though now he fleets like any rook
Across the fields to Anne."

And I am sure, that on some hour
Coquetting soft 'twixt sun and shower,
He stooped and broke a daisy-flower
With heart of tiny span,
And bore it as a lover's dower
Across the fields to Anne.

While from her cottage garden-bed
She plucked a jasmine's goodlihede,
To scent his jerkin's brown instead;
Now since that love began,
What luckier swain than he who sped
Across the fields to Anne?

The winding path whereon I pace,
The hedgerow's green, the summer's grace,
Are still before me face to face;
Methinks I almost can
Turn poet and join the singing race
Across the fields to Anne!

Richard Burton.

THE HOUSE AND THE ROAD

The little Road says, Go,
The little House says, Stay:
And O, it's bonny here at home,
But I must go away.

The little Road, like me,
Would seek and turn and know;
And forth I must, to learn the things
The little Road would show!

And go I must, my dears,
And journey while I may,
Though heart be sore for the little House
That had no word but Stay.

Maybe, no other way
Your child could ever know
Why a little House would have you stay,
When a little Road says, Go.

Josephine Preston Peabody.

THE PATH TO THE WOODS

Its friendship and its carelessness
Did lead me many a mile,
Through goat's-rue, with its dim caress,
And pink and pearl-white smile;
Through crowfoot, with its golden lure,
And promise of far things,
And sorrel with its glance demure
And wide-eyed wonderings.

It led me with its innocence,
As childhood leads the wise,
With elbows here of tattered fence,
And blue of wildflower eyes;
With whispers low of leafy speech,
And brook-sweet utterance;
With bird-like words of oak and beech,
And whisperings clear as Pan's.

It led me with its childlike charm,
As candor leads desire,
Now with a clasp of blossomy arm,
A butterfly kiss of fire;
Now with a toss of tousled gold,
A barefoot sound of green,

A breath of musk, of mossy mold,
With vague allurements keen.

It led me with remembered things
Into an old-time vale,
Peopled with faëry glimmerings,
And flower-like fancies pale;
Where fungous forms stood, gold and gray,
Each in its mushroom gown,
And, roofed with red, glimpsed far away,
A little toadstool town.

It led me with an idle ease,
A vagabond look and air,
A sense of ragged arms and knees
In weeds grown everywhere;
It led me, as a gypsy leads,
To dingles no one knows,
With beauty burred with thorny seeds,
And tangled wild with rose.

It led me as simplicity
Leads age and its demands,
With bee-beat of its ecstasy,
And berry-stained touch of hands;
With round revealments, puff-ball white,
Through rents of weedy brown,
And petaled movements of delight
In roseleaf limb and gown.

It led me on and on and on,
Beyond the Far Away,
Into a world long dead and gone, —

The world of Yesterday:
A faëry world of memory,
Old with its hills and streams,
Wherein the child I used to be
Still wanders with his dreams.

Madison Cawein.

SOMETIMES

ACROSS the fields of yesterday
He sometimes comes to me,
A little lad just back from play —
The lad I used to be.

And yet he smiles so wistfully
Once he has crept within,
I wonder if he hopes to see
The man I might have been.

Thomas S. Jones, Jr.

RENASCENCE

ALL I could see from where I stood
Was three long mountains and a wood;
I turned and looked another way,
And saw three islands in a bay.
So with my eyes I traced the line
Of the horizon, thin and fine,
Straight around till I was come
Back to where I'd started from;
And all I saw from where I stood
Was three long mountains and a wood.

Over these things I could not see;
These were the things that bounded me;
And I could touch them with my hand,
Almost, I thought, from where I stand.
And all at once things seemed so small
My breath came short, and scarce at all.
But, sure, the sky is big, I said;
Miles and miles above my head;
So here upon my back I'll lie
And look my fill into the sky.
And so I looked, and, after all,
The sky was not so very tall.
The sky, I said, must somewhere stop,
And — sure enough! — I see the top!
The sky, I thought, is not so grand;
I 'most could touch it with my hand!
And, reaching up my hand to try,
I screamed to feel it touch the sky.

I screamed, and — lo! — Infinity
Came down and settled over me;
And, pressing of the Undefined
The definition on my mind,
Held up before my eyes a glass
Through which my shrinking sight did pass
Until it seemed I must behold
Immensity made manifold;
Whispered to me a word whose sound
Deafened the air for worlds around,
And brought unmuffled to my ears
The gossiping of friendly spheres,
The creaking of the tented sky,
The ticking of Eternity.

I saw and heard, and knew at last
The How and Why of all things, past,
And present, and forevermore.
The universe, cleft to the core,
Lay open to my probing sense
That, sick'ning, I would fain pluck thence
But could not, — nay! But needs must suck
At the great wound, and could not pluck
My lips away till I had drawn
All venom out. — Ah, fearful pawn!
For my omniscience paid I toll
In infinite remorse of soul.
All sin was of my sinning, all
Atoning mine, and mine the gall
Of all regret. Mine was the weight
Of every brooded wrong, the hate
That stood behind each envious thrust,
Mine every greed, mine every lust.
And all the while for every grief,
Each suffering, I craved relief
With individual desire, —
Craved all in vain! And felt fierce fire
About a thousand people crawl;
Perished with each, — then mourned for all!
A man was starving in Capri;
He moved his eyes and looked at me;
I felt his gaze, I heard his moan,
And knew his hunger as my own.
I saw at sea a great fog-bank
Between two ships that struck and sank;
A thousand screams the heavens smote;
And every scream tore through my throat.
No hurt I did not feel, no death

That was not mine; mine each last breath
That, crying, met an answering cry
From the compassion that was I.
All suffering mine, and mine its rod;
Mine, pity like the pity of God.
Ah, awful weight! Infinity
Pressed down upon the finite Me!
My anguished spirit, like a bird,
Beating against my lips I heard;
Yet lay the weight so close about
There was no room for it without.
And so beneath the Weight lay I
And suffered death, but could not die.

Long had I lain thus, craving death,
When quietly the earth beneath
Gave way, and inch by inch, so great
At last had grown the crushing weight,
Into the earth I sank till I
Full six feet under ground did lie,
And sank no more, — there is no weight
Can follow here, however great.
From off my breast I felt it roll,
And as it went my tortured soul
Burst forth and fled in such a gust
That all about me swirled the dust.

Deep in the earth I rested now;
Cool is its hand upon the brow
And soft its breast beneath the head
Of one who is so gladly dead.
And all at once, and over all,
The pitying rain began to fall;

I lay and heard each pattering hoof
Upon my lowly, thatchèd roof,
And seemed to love the sound far more
Than ever I had done before.
For rain it hath a friendly sound
To one who's six feet underground;
And scarce the friendly voice or face:
A grave is such a quiet place.

The rain, I said, is kind to come
And speak to me in my new home.
I would I were alive again
To kiss the fingers of the rain,
To drink into my eyes the shine
Of every slanting silver line,
To catch the freshened, fragrant breeze
From drenched and dripping apple-trees.
For soon the shower will be done,
And then the broad face of the sun
Will laugh above the rain-soaked earth
Until the world with answering mirth
Shakes joyously, and each round drop
Rolls, twinkling, from its grass-blade top.
How can I bear it; buried here,
While overhead the sky grows clear
And blue again after the storm?
O, multi-colored, multiform,
Beloved beauty over me,
That I shall never, never see
Again! Spring-silver, autumn-gold,
That I shall never more behold!
Sleeping your myriad magics through,
Close-sepulchred away from you!

O God, I cried, give me new birth,
And put me back upon the earth!
Upset each cloud's gigantic gourd
And let the heavy rain, down-poured
In one big torrent, set me free,
Washing my grave away from me!

I ceased; and, through the breathless hush
That answered me, the far-off rush
Of herald wings came whispering
Like music down the vibrant string
Of my ascending prayer, and — crash!
Before the wild wind's whistling lash
The startled storm-clouds reared on high
And plunged in terror down the sky,
And the big rain in one black wave
Fell from the sky and struck my grave.

I know not how such things can be
I only know there came to me
A fragrance such as never clings
To aught save happy living things;
A sound as of some joyous elf
Singing sweet songs to please himself,
And, through and over everything,
A sense of glad awakening.
The grass, a-tiptoe at my ear,
Whispering to me I could hear;
I felt the rain's cool finger-tips
Brushed tenderly across my lips,
Laid gently on my sealèd sight,
And all at once the heavy night
Fell from my eyes and I could see, —

A drenched and dripping apple-tree,
A last long line of silver rain,
A sky grown clear and blue again.
And as I looked a quickening gust
Of wind blew up to me and thrust
Into my face a miracle
Of orchard-breath, and with the smell, —
I know not how such things can be! —
I breathed my soul back into me.
Ah! Up then from the ground sprang I
And hailed the earth with such a cry
As is not heard save from a man
Who has been dead, and lives again.
About the trees my arms I wound;
Like one gone mad I hugged the ground;
I raised my quivering arms on high;
I laughed and laughed into the sky,
Till at my throat a strangling sob
Caught fiercely, and a great heart-throb
Sent instant tears into my eyes;
O God, I cried, no dark disguise
Can e'er hereafter hide from me
Thy radiant identity!
Thou canst not move across the grass
But my quick eyes will see Thee pass,
Nor speak, however silently,
But my hushed voice will answer Thee.
I know the path that tells Thy way
Through the cool eve of every day;
God, I can push the grass apart
And lay my finger on Thy heart!

The world stands out on either side
No wider than the heart is wide;

Above the world is stretched the sky, —
No higher than the soul is high.
The heart can push the sea and land
Farther away on either hand;
The soul can split the sky in two,
And let the face of God shine through.
But East and West will pinch the heart
That cannot keep them pushed apart;
And he whose soul is flat — the sky
Will cave in on him by and by.

Edna St. Vincent Millay.

SOULS

My Soul goes clad in gorgeous things,
  Scarlet and gold and blue;
And at her shoulder sudden wings
  Like long flames flicker through.

And she is swallow-fleet, and free
  From mortal bonds and bars.
She laughs, because Eternity
  Blossoms for her with stars!

O folk who scorn my stiff gray gown,
  My dull and foolish face, —
Can ye not see my Soul flash down,
  A singing flame through space?

And folk, whose earth-stained looks I hate,
  Why may I not divine
Your Souls, that must be passionate,
  Shining and swift, as mine!

Fannie Stearns Davis.

FIAT LUX

THEN that dread angel near the awful throne,
Leaving the seraphs ranged in flaming tiers,
Winged his dark way through those unpinioned spheres,
And on the void's black beetling edge, alone,
Stood with raised wings, and listened for the tone
Of God's command to reach his eager ears,
While Chaos wavered, for she felt her years
Unsceptered now in that convulsive zone.
Night trembled. And as one hath oft beheld
A lamp within a vase light up its gloom,
So God's voice lighted him, from heel to plume:
"Let there be light!" It said, and Darkness, quelled,
Shrunk noiseless backward in her monstrous womb
Through vasts unwinnowed by the wings of eld!

Lloyd Mifflin.

THE DREAMER

"*Why do you seek the sun,*
In your Bubble-Crown ascending?
Your chariot will melt to mist,
Your crown will have an ending."
"Nay, sun is but a Bubble,
Earth is a whiff of Foam —
To my caves on the coast of Thule
Each night I call them home.
Thence Faiths blow forth to angels
And Loves blow forth to men —
They break and turn to nothing
And I make them whole again:

On the crested waves of chaos
I ride them back reborn:
New stars I bring at evening
For those that burst at morn:
My soul is the wind of Thule
And evening is the sign,
The sun is but a Bubble,
A fragile child of mine."

Nicholas Vachel Lindsay.

A CARAVAN FROM CHINA COMES

(*After Hafiz*)

A CARAVAN from China comes;
  For miles it sweetens all the air
With fragrant silks and dreaming gums,
  Attar and myrrh —
A caravan from China comes.

O merchant, tell me what you bring,
  With music sweet of camel bells;
How long have you been travelling
  With these sweet smells?
O merchant, tell me what you bring.

A lovely lady is my freight,
  A lock escaped of her long hair, —
That is this perfume delicate
  That fills the air —
A lovely lady is my freight.

Her face is from another land,
  I think she is no mortal maid, —

Her beauty, like some ghostly hand,
  Makes me afraid;
Her face is from another land.

The little moon my cargo is,
  About her neck the Pleiades
Clasp hands and sing; Hafiz, 't is this
  Perfumes the breeze —
The little moon my cargo is.

Richard Le Gallienne.

AS I CAME DOWN FROM LEBANON

As I came down from Lebanon,
Came winding, wandering slowly down
Through mountain passes bleak and brown,
The cloudless day was well-nigh done.
The city, like an opal set
In emerald, showed each minaret
Afire with radiant beams of sun,
And glistened orange, fig, and lime,
Where song-birds made melodious chime,
As I came down from Lebanon.

As I came down from Lebanon,
Like lava in the dying glow,
Through olive orchards far below
I saw the murmuring river run;
And 'neath the wall upon the sand
Swart sheiks from distant Samarcand,
With precious spices they had won,
Lay long and languidly in wait
Till they might pass the guarded gate,
As I came down from Lebanon.

As I came down from Lebanon,
I saw strange men from lands afar,
In mosque and square and gay bazar,
The Magi that the Moslem shun,
And grave Effendi from Stamboul,
Who sherbet sipped in corners cool;
And, from the balconies o'errun
With roses, gleamed the eyes of those
Who dwell in still seraglios,
As I came down from Lebanon.

As I came down from Lebanon,
The flaming flower of daytime died,
And Night, arrayed as is a bride
Of some great king, in garments spun
Of purple and the finest gold,
Outbloomed in glories manifold,
Until the moon, above the dun
And darkening desert, void of shade,
Shone like a keen Damascus blade,
As I came down from Lebanon.

Clinton Scollard.

THE ONLY WAY

I

Memphis and Karnak, Luxor, Thebes, the Nile:
Of these your letters told; and I who read
Saw loom on dim horizons Egypt's dead
In march across the desert, mile on mile,
A ghostly caravan in slow defile
Between the sand and stars; and at their head
From unmapped darkness into darkness fled
The gods that Egypt feared a little while.

There black against the night I saw them loom
  With captive kings and armies in array
Remembered only by their scupltured doom,
  And thought: What Egypt was are we to-day.
Then rose obscure against the rearward gloom
  The march of Empires yet to pass away.

II

I looked in vision down the centuries
  And saw how Athens stood a sunlit while
  A sovereign city free from greed and guile,
The half-embodied dream of Pericles.
Then saw I one of smooth words, swift to please,
  At laggard virtue mock with shrug and smile;
  With Cleon's creed rang court and peristyle,
Then sank the sun in far Sicilian seas.

From brows ignoble fell the violet crown.
  Again the warning sounds; the hosts engage:
  In Cleon's face we fling our battle gage,
We win as foes of Cleon loud renown;
  But while we think to build the coming age
The laurel on our brows is turning brown.

III

We top the poisonous blooms that choke the state,
  At flower and fruit our flashing strokes are made,
  The whetted scythe on stalk and stem is laid,
But deeper must we strike to extirpate
The rooted evil that within our gate
  Will sprout again and flourish, branch and blade;
  For only from within can ill be stayed
While Adam's seed is unregenerate.

With zeal redoubled let our strength be strained
  To cut the rooted causes where they hold,
  Nor spend our sinews on the fungus mold
When all the breeding marshes must be drained.
  Be this our aim; and let our youth be trained
  To honor virtue more than place and gold.

IV

A hundred cities sapped by slow decay,
  A hundred codes and systems proven vain
  Lie hearsed in sand upon the heaving plain,
Memorial ruins mounded, still and gray;
And we who plod the barren waste to-day
  Another code evolving, think to gain
  Surcease of man's inheritance of pain
And mold a state immune from evil's sway.

Not laws; but virtue in the soul we need,
  The old Socratic justice in the heart,
The golden rule become the people's creed
  When years of training have performed their part:
  For thus alone in home and church and mart
Can evil perish and the race be freed.

Louis V. Ledoux.

THE DUST DETHRONED

SARGON is dust, Semiramis a clod!
  In crypts profaned the moon at midnight peers;
  The owl upon the Sphinx hoots in her ears,
And scant and sear the desert grasses nod
Where once the armies of Assyria trod,

With younger sunlight splendid on the spears;
The lichens cling the closer with the years,
And seal the eyelids of the weary god.

Where high the tombs of royal Egypt heave,
The vulture shadows with arrested wings
The indecipherable boast of kings,
As Arab children hear their mother's cry
And leave in mockery their toy — they leave
The skull of Pharaoh staring at the sky.

George Sterling.

KINCHINJUNGA

(Which is the next highest of mountains)

I

O WHITE Priest of Eternity, around
Whose lofty summit veiling clouds arise
Of the earth's immemorial sacrifice
To Brahma in whose breath all lives and dies;
O Hierarch enrobed in timeless snows,
First-born of Asia whose maternal throes
Seem changed now to a million human woes,
Holy thou art and still! Be so, nor sound
One sigh of all the mystery in thee found.

II

For in this world too much is overclear,
Immortal Ministrant to many lands,
From whose ice-altars flow to fainting sands
Rivers that each libation poured expands.

Too much is known, O Ganges-giving sire!
Thy people fathom life and find it dire,
Thy people fathom death, and, in it, fire
To live again, though in Illusion's sphere,
Behold concealed as Grief is in a tear.

III

Wherefore continue, still enshrined, thy rites,
Though dark Thibet, that dread ascetic, falls
In strange austerity, whose trance appalls,
Before thee, and a suppliant on thee calls.
Continue still thy silence high and sure,
That something beyond fleeting may endure —
Something that shall forevermore allure
Imagination on to mystic flights
Wherein alone no wing of Evil lights.

IV

Yea, wrap thy awful gulfs and acolytes
Of lifted granite round with reachless snows.
Stand for Eternity while pilgrim rows
Of all the nations envy thy repose.
Ensheath thy swart sublimities, unscaled.
Be that alone on earth which has not failed.
Be that which never yet has yearned or ailed,
But since primeval Power upreared thy heights
Has stood above all deaths and all delights.

V

And though thy loftier Brother shall be King,
High-priest art thou to Brahma unrevealed,
While thy white sanctity forever sealed

In icy silence leaves desire congealed.
In ghostly ministrations to the sun,
And to the mendicant stars and the moon-nun,
Be holy still, till East to West has run,
And till no sacrificial suffering
On any shrine is left to tell life's sting.

Cale Young Rice.

"SCUM O' THE EARTH"

I

At the gate of the West I stand,
On the isle where the nations throng.
We call them "scum o' the earth";

Stay, are we doing you wrong,
Young fellow from Socrates' land? —
You, like a Hermes so lissome and strong
Fresh from the Master Praxiteles' hand?
So you're of Spartan birth?
Descended, perhaps, from one of the band —
Deathless in story and song —
Who combed their long hair at Thermopylæ's pass?
Ah, I forget the straits, alas!
More tragic than theirs, more compassion-worth,
That have doomed you to march in our "immigrant
class"
Where you 're nothing but "scum o' the earth."

II

You Pole with the child on your knee,
What dower bring you to the land of the free?

Hark! does she croon
That sad little tune
That Chopin once found on his Polish lea
And mounted in gold for you and for me?
Now a ragged young fiddler answers
In wild Czech melody
That Dvořak took whole from the dancers.
And the heavy faces bloom
In the wonderful Slavic way;
The little, dull eyes, the brows a-gloom,
Suddenly dawn like the day.
While, watching these folk and their mystery,
I forget that they're nothing worth;
That Bohemians, Slovaks, Croatians,
And men of all Slavic nations
Are "polacks" — and "scum o' the earth."

III

Genoese boy of the level brow,
Lad of the lustrous, dreamy eyes
A-stare at Manhattan's pinnacles now
In the first sweet shock of a hushed surprise;
Within your far-rapt seer's eyes
I catch the glow of the wild surmise
That played on the Santa Maria's prow
In that still gray dawn,
Four centuries gone,
When a world from the wave began to rise.
Oh, it's hard to foretell what high emprise
Is the goal that gleams
When Italy's dreams
Spread wing and sweep into the skies.

Cæsar dreamed him a world ruled well;
Dante dreamed Heaven out of Hell;
Angelo brought us there to dwell;
And you, are you of a different birth? —
You're only a "dago," — and "scum o' the earth"!

IV

Stay, are we doing you wrong
Calling you "scum o' the earth,"
Man of the sorrow-bowed head,
Of the features tender yet strong, —
Man of the eyes full of wisdom and mystery
Mingled with patience and dread?
Have not I known you in history,
Sorrow-bowed head?
Were you the poet-king, worth
Treasures of Ophir unpriced?
Were you the prophet, perchance, whose art
Foretold how the rabble would mock
That shepherd of spirits, erelong,
Who should carry the lambs on his heart
And tenderly feed his flock?
Man — lift that sorrow-bowed head.
Lo! 't is the face of the Christ!

The vision dies at its birth.
You're merely a butt for our mirth.
You're a "sheeny" — and therefore despised
And rejected as "scum o' the earth."

V

Countrymen, bend and invoke
Mercy for us blasphemers,

For that we spat on these marvelous folk,
Nations of darers and dreamers,
Scions of singers and seers,
Our peers, and more than our peers.
"Rabble and refuse," we name them
And "scum o' the earth," to shame them.
Mercy for us of the few, young years,
Of the culture so callow and crude,
Of the hands so grasping and rude,
The lips so ready for sneers
At the sons of our ancient more-than-peers.
Mercy for us who dare despise
Men in whose loins our Homer lies;
Mothers of men who shall bring to us
The glory of Titian, the grandeur of Huss;
Children in whose frail arms shall rest
Prophets and singers and saints of the West.

Newcomers all from the eastern seas,
Help us incarnate dreams like these.
Forget, and forgive, that we did you wrong.
Help us to father a nation, strong
In the comradeship of an equal birth,
In the wealth of the richest bloods of earth.

Robert Haven Schauffler.

DA BOY FROM ROME

To-day ees com' from Eetaly
  A boy ees leeve een Rome,
An' he ees stop an' speak weeth me —
  I weesh he stay at home.

He stop an' say "Hallo," to me.
  An' w'en he standin' dere
I smal da smal of Eetaly
  Steell steeckin' een hees hair,
Dat com' weeth heem across da sea,
  An' een da clo'es he wear.

Da peopla bomp heem een da street,
  Da noise ees scare heem, too;
He ees so clumsy een da feet
  He don't know w'at to do,
Dere ees so many theeng he meet
  Dat ees so strange, so new.

He sheever an' he ask eef here
  Eet ees so always cold.
Den een hees eye ees com' a tear —
  He ees no vera old —
An', oh, hees voice ees soun' so queer
  I have no heart for scold.

He look up een da sky so gray,
  But oh, hees eye ees be
So far away, so far away,
  An' w'at he see I see.
Da sky eet ees no gray to-day
  At home een Eetaly.

He see da glada peopla seet
  Where warma shine da sky —
Oh, while he eesa look at eet
  He ees baygeen to cry.
Eef I no growl an' swear a beet
  So, too, my frand, would I.

Oh, why he stop an' speak weeth me,
  Dees boy dat leeve een Rome,
An' com' to-day from Eetaly?
  I weesh he stay at home.

Thomas Augustine Daly.

THE FUGITIVES

We are they that go, that go,
Plunging before the hidden blow.
We run the byways of the earth,
For we are fugitive from birth,
Blindfolded, with wide hands abroad
That sow, that sow the sullen sod.

We cannot wait, we cannot stop
For flushing field or quickened crop;
The orange bow of dusky dawn
Glimmers our smoking swath upon;
Blindfolded still we hurry on.

How we do know the ways we run
That are blindfolded from the sun?
We stagger swiftly to the call,
Our wide hands feeling for the wall.

Oh, ye who climb to some clear heaven,
By grace of day and leisure given,
Pity us, fugitive and driven —
The lithe whip curling on our track,
The headlong haste that looks not back!

Florence Wilkinson.

THE SONG OF THE UNSUCCESSFUL

WE are the toilers from whom God barred
  The gifts that are good to hold.
We meant full well and we tried full hard,
  And our failures were manifold.

And we are the clan of those whose kin
  Were a millstone dragging them down.
Yea, we had to sweat for our brother's sin,
  And lose the victor's crown.

The seeming-able, who all but scored,
  From their teeming tribe we come:
What was there wrong with us, O Lord,
  That our lives were dark and dumb?

The men ten-talented, who still
  Strangely missed of the goal,
Of them we are: it seems Thy will
  To harrow some in soul.

We are the sinners, too, whose lust
  Conquered the higher claims,
We sat us prone in the common dust,
  And played at the devil's games.

We are the hard-luck folk, who strove
  Zealously, but in vain;
We lost and lost, while our comrades throve,
  And still we lost again.

We are the doubles of those whose way
  Was festal with fruits and flowers;

Body and brain we were sound as they,
  But the prizes were not ours.

A mighty army our full ranks make,
  We shake the graves as we go;
The sudden stroke and the slow heartbreak,
  They both have brought us low.

And while we are laying life's sword aside,
  Spent and dishonored and sad,
Our epitaph this, when once we have died:
  "The weak lie here, and the bad."

We wonder if this can be really the close,
  Life's fever cooled by death's trance;
And we cry, though it seem to our dearest of foes,
  "God, give us another chance!"

Richard Burton.

THEY WENT FORTH TO BATTLE, BUT THEY ALWAYS FELL

THEY went forth to battle, but they always fell;
  Their eyes were fixed above the sullen shields;
Nobly they fought and bravely, but not well,
And sank heart-wounded by a subtle spell.
  They knew not fear that to the foeman yields,
  They were not weak, as one who vainly wields
A futile weapon; yet the sad scrolls tell
How on the hard-fought field they always fell.

It was a secret music that they heard,
  A sad sweet plea for pity and for peace;

And that which pierced the heart was but a word,
Though the white breast was red-lipped where the sword
  Pressed a fierce cruel kiss, to put surcease
  On its hot thirst, but drank a hot increase.
Ah, they by some strange troubling doubt were stirred,
And died for hearing what no foeman heard.

They went forth to battle but they always fell;
  Their might was not the might of lifted spears;
Over the battle-clamor came a spell
Of troubling music, and they fought not well.
  Their wreaths are willows and their tribute, tears;
  Their names are old sad stories in men's ears;
Yet they will scatter the red hordes of Hell,
Who went to battle forth and always fell.

Shaemas O Sheel.

THE EAGLE THAT IS FORGOTTEN

(*John P. Altgeld*)

SLEEP softly . . . eagle forgotten . . . under the stone.
Time has its way with you there, and the clay has its own.
"We have buried him now," thought your foes, and in secret rejoiced.
They made a brave show of their mourning, their hatred unvoiced.
They had snarled at you, barked at you, foamed at you, day after day.
Now you were ended. They praised you . . . and laid you away.
The others, that mourned you in silence and terror and truth,

The widow bereft of her crust, and the boy without
youth,
The mocked and the scorned and the wounded, the
lame and the poor,
That should have remembered forever, . . . remember
no more.
Where are those lovers of yours, on what name do they
call,
The lost, that in armies wept over your funeral pall?
They call on the names of a hundred high-valiant
ones,
A hundred white eagles have risen, the sons of your
sons.
The zeal in their wings is a zeal that your dreaming
began,
The valor that wore out your soul in the service of man.
Sleep softly . . . eagle forgotten . . . under the stone.
Time has its way with you there, and the clay has its
own.
Sleep on, O brave-hearted, O wise man that kindled
the flame —
To live in mankind is far more than to live in a name,
To live in mankind, far, far more than to live in a
name! —

Nicholas Vachel Lindsay.

A MEMORIAL TABLET

Oh, Agathocles, fare thee well!

NAKED and brave thou goest
Without one glance behind!
Hast thou no fear, Agathocles,
Or backward grief of mind?

The dreamy dog beside thee
  Presses against thy knee;
He, too, oh, sweet Agathocles,
  Is deaf and visioned like thee.

Thou art so lithe and lovely
  And yet thou art not ours.
What Delphic saying compels thee
  Of kings or topless towers?

That little blowing mantle
  Thou losest from thine arm —
No shoon nor staff, Agathocles,
  Nor sword, to fend from harm!

Thou hast the changed impersonal
  Awed brow of mystery —
Yesterday thou wast burning,
  Mad boy, for Glaucöe.

Philis thy mother calls thee:
  Mine eyes with tears are dim,
Turn once, look once, Agathocles —
  (*The gods have blinded him.*)

Come back, Agathocles, the night —
  Brings thee what place of rest?
Wine-sweet are Glaucöe's kisses,
  Flower-soft her budding breast.

He seems to hearken, Glaucöe,
  He seems to listen and smile;
(*Nay, Philis, but a god-song*
  He follows this many a mile.)

Come back, come back, Agathocles!
(He scents the asphodel;
Unearthly swift he runneth.)
Agathocles, farewell!

Florence Wilkinson.

TO-DAY

VOICE, with what emulous fire thou singest free hearts of old fashion,
English scorners of Spain, sweeping the blue sea-way,
Sing me the daring of life for life, the magnanimous passion
Of man for man in the mean populous streets of To-day!

Hand, with what color and power thou couldst show, in the ring hot-sanded,
Brown Bestiarius holding the lean tawn tiger at bay,
Paint me the wrestle of Toil with the wild-beast Want, bare-handed;
Shadow me forth a soul steadily facing To-day!

Helen Gray Cone.

THE MAN WITH THE HOE

(Written after seeing Millet's world-famous painting)

BOWED by the weight of centuries he leans
Upon his hoe and gazes on the ground,
The emptiness of ages in his face,
And on his back the burden of the world.
Who made him dead to rapture and despair,
A thing that grieves not and that never hopes,

Stolid and stunned, a brother to the ox?
Who loosened and let down this brutal jaw?
Whose was the hand that slanted back this brow?
Whose breath blew out the light within this brain?
Is this the Thing the Lord God made and gave
To have dominion over sea and land;
To trace the stars and search the heavens for power;
To feel the passion of Eternity?
Is this the Dream He dreamed who shaped the suns
And marked their ways upon the ancient deep?
Down all the stretch of Hell to its last gulf
There is no shape more terrible than this —
More tongued with censure of the world's blind greed —
More filled with signs and portents for the soul —
More fraught with menace to the universe.

What gulfs between him and the seraphim!
Slave of the wheel of labor, what to him
Are Plato and the swing of Pleiades?
What the long reaches of the peaks of song,
The rift of dawn, the reddening of the rose?
Through this dread shape the suffering ages look;
Time's tragedy is in that aching stoop;
Through this dread shape humanity betrayed,
Plundered, profaned and disinherited,
Cries protest to the Judges of the World,
A protest that is also prophecy.

O masters, lords and rulers in all lands,
Is this the handiwork you give to God,
This monstrous thing distorted and soul-quenched?
How will you ever straighten up this shape;

Touch it again with immortality;
Give back the upward looking and the light;
Rebuild in it the music and the dream;
Make right the immemorial infamies,
Perfidious wrongs, immedicable woes?

O masters, lords and rulers in all lands,
How will the Future reckon with this Man?
How answer his brute question in that hour
When whirlwinds of rebellion shake the world?
How will it be with kingdoms and with kings —
With those who shaped him to the thing he is —
When this dumb Terror shall reply to God,
After the silence of the centuries?

Edwin Markham.

EXORDIUM

SPEAK! said my soul, be stern and adequate;
The sunset falls from Heaven, the year is late,
Love waits with fallen tresses at thy gate
And mourns for perished days.
Speak! in the rigor of thy fate and mine,
Ere these scant, dying days, bright-lipped with wine,
All one by one depart, resigned, divine;
Through desert, autumn ways.

Speak! thou art lonely in thy chilly mind,
With all this desperate solitude of wind,
The solitude of tears that make thee blind,
Of wild and causeless tears.
Speak! thou hast need of me, heart, hand and head,
Speak, if it be an echo of thy dread,

A dirge of hope, of young illusions dead —
Perchance God hears!

George Cabot Lodge.

THE FROZEN GRAIL

(To Peary and his men, before the last expedition)

Why sing the legends of the Holy Grail,
The dead crusaders of the Sepulchre,
While these men live? Are the great bards all dumb?
Here is a vision to shake the blood of Song,
And make Fame's watchman tremble at his post.

What shall prevail against the spirit of man,
When cold, the lean and snarling wolf of hunger,
The threatening spear of ice-mailed Solitude,
Silence, and space, and ghostly-footed Fear
Prevail not? Dante, in his frozen hell
Shivering, endured no bleakness like the void
These men have warmed with their own flaming will,
And peopled with their dreams. The wind from fierce
Arcturus in their faces, at their backs
The whip of the world's doubt, and in their souls
Courage to die — if death shall be the price
Of that cold cup that will assuage their thirst;
They climb, and fall, and stagger toward the goal.
They lay themselves the road whereby they travel,
And sue God for a franchise. Does He watch
Behind the lattice of the boreal lights?
In that grail-chapel of their stern-vowed quest,
Ninety of God's long paces toward the North,
Will they behold the splendor of His face?

To conquer the world must man renounce the world?
These have renounced it. Had ye only faith
Ye might move mountains, said the Nazarene.
Why, these have faith to move the zones of man
Out to the point where All and Nothing meet.
They catch the bit of Death between their teeth,
In one wild dash to trample the unknown
And leap the gates of knowledge. They have dared
Even to defy the sentinel that guards
The doors of the forbidden — dared to hurl
Their breathing bodies after the Ideal,
That like the heavenly kingdom must be taken
Only by violence. The star that leads
The leader of this quest has held the world
True to its orbit for a million years.

And shall he fail? They never fail who light
Their lamp of faith at the unwavering flame
Burnt for the altar service of the Race
Since the beginning. He shall find the strange —
The white immaculate Virgin of the North,
Whose steady gaze no mortal ever dared,
Whose icy hand no human ever grasped.
In the dread silence and the solitude
She waits and listens through the centuries
For one indomitable, destined soul,
Born to endure the glory of her eyes,
And lift his warm lips to the frozen Grail.

Elsa Barker.

THE UNCONQUERED AIR

I

OTHERS endure Man's rule: he therefore deems
  I shall endure it — I, the unconquered Air!
  Imagines this triumphant strength may bear
His paltry sway! yea, ignorantly dreams,
Because proud Rhea now his vassal seems,
  And Neptune him obeys in billowy lair,
  That he a more sublime assault may dare,
Where blown by tempest wild the vulture screams!

Presumptuous, he mounts: I toss his bones
  Back from the height supernal he has braved:
Ay, as his vessel nears my perilous zones,
I blow the cockle-shell away like chaff
  And give him to the Sea he has enslaved.
He founders in its depths; and then I laugh!

II

Impregnable I held myself, secure
  Against intrusion. Who can measure Man?
  How should I guess his mortal will outran
Defeat so far that danger could allure
For its own sake? — that he would all endure,
  All sacrifice, all suffer, rather than
  Forego the daring dreams Olympian
That prophesy to him of victory sure?

Ah, tameless courage! — dominating power
That, all attempting, in a deathless hour
  Made earth-born Titans godlike, in revolt! —

Fear is the fire that melts Icarian wings:
Who fears nor Fate, nor Time, nor what Time brings,
  May drive Apollo's steeds, or wield the thunderbolt!

Florence Earle Coates.

THE HAPPIEST HEART

WHO drives the horses of the sun
  Shall lord it but a day;
Better the lowly deed were done,
  And kept the humble way.

The rust will find the sword of fame,
  The dust will hide the crown;
Ay, none shall nail so high his name
  Time will not tear it down.

The happiest heart that ever beat
  Was in some quiet breast
That found the common daylight sweet,
  And left to Heaven the rest.

John Vance Cheney.

TO A NEW YORK SHOP-GIRL DRESSED FOR SUNDAY

TO-DAY I saw the shop-girl go
Down gay Broadway to meet her beau.

Conspicuous, splendid, conscious, sweet,
She spread abroad and took the street.

And all that niceness would forbid,
Superb, she smiled upon and did.

Let other girls, whose happier days
Preserve the perfume of their ways,

Go modestly. The passing hour
Adds splendor to their opening flower.

But from this child too swift a doom
Must steal her prettiness and bloom,

Toil and weariness hide the grace
That pleads a moment from her face.

So blame her not if for a day
She flaunts her glories while she may.

She half perceives, half understands,
Snatching her gifts with both her hands.

The little strut beneath the skirt
That lags neglected in the dirt,

The indolent swagger down the street —
Who can condemn such happy feet!

Innocent! vulgar — that's the truth!
Yet with the darling wiles of youth!

The bright, self-conscious eyes that stare
With such hauteur, beneath such hair!
Perhaps the men will find me fair!

Charming and charmed, flippant, arrayed,
Fluttered and foolish, proud, displayed,
Infinite pathos of parade!

The bangles and the narrowed waist —
The tinsled boa — forgive the taste!
Oh, the starved nights she gave for that,
And bartered bread to buy her hat!

She flows before the reproachful sage
And begs her woman's heritage.

Dear child, with the defiant eyes,
Insolent with the half surmise
We do not quite admire, I know
How foresight frowns on this vain show!

And judgment, wearily sad, may see
No grace in such frivolity.

Yet which of us was ever bold
To worship Beauty, hungry and cold!

Scorn famine down, proudly expressed
Apostle to what things are best.

Let him who starves to buy the food
For his soul's comfort find her good,

Nor chide the frills and furbelows
That are the prettiest things she knows.

Poet and prophet in God's eyes
Make no more perfect sacrifice.

Who knows before what inner shrine
She eats with them the bread and wine?

Poor waif! One of the sacred few
That madly sought the best they knew!

Dear — let me lean my cheek to-night
Close, close to yours. Ah, that is right.

How warm and near! At last I see
One beauty shines for thee and me.

So let us love and understand —
Whose hearts are hidden in God's hand.

And we will cherish your brief Spring
And all its fragile flowering.

God loves all prettiness, and on this
Surely his angels lay their kiss.

Anna Hempstead Branch.

A FAUN IN WALL STREET

WHAT shape so furtive steals along the dim
Bleak street, barren of throngs, this day of June;
This day of rest, when all the roses swoon
In Attic vales where dryads wait for him?
What sylvan this, and what the stranger whim
That lured him here this golden afternoon;
Ways where the dusk has fallen oversoon
In the deep canyon, torrentless and grim?

Great Pan is far, O mad estray, and these
  Bare walls that leap to heaven and hide the skies
Are fanes men rear to other deities;
  Far to the east the haunted woodland lies,
And cloudless still, from cyclad-dotted seas,
  Hymettus and the hills of Hellas rise.

John Myers O'Hara.

THE MYSTIC

By seven vineyards on one hill
  We walked. The native wine
In clusters grew beside us two,
  For your lips and for mine,

When, "Hark!" you said, — "Was that a bell
  Or a bubbling spring we heard?"
But I was wise and closed my eyes
  And listened to a bird;

For as summer leaves are bent and shake
  With singers passing through,
So moves in me continually
  The wingèd breath of you.

You tasted from a single vine
  And took from that your fill —
But I inclined to every kind,
  All seven on one hill.

Witter Bynner.

THE CLOUD

THE islands called me far away,
  The valleys called me home.
The rivers with a silver voice
  Drew on my heart to come.

The paths reached tendrils to my hair
  From every vine and tree.
There was no refuge anywhere
  Until I came to thee.

There is a northern cloud I know,
  Along a mountain crest;
And as she folds her wings of mist,
  So I could make my rest.

There is no chain to bind her so
  Unto that purple height;
And she will shine and wander, slow,
  Slow, with a cloud's delight.

Would she begone? She melts away,
  A heavenly joyous thing.
Yet day will find the mountain white,
  White-folded with her wing.

As you may see, but half aware
  If it be late or soon,
Soft breathing on the day-time air,
  The fair forgotten Moon.

And though love cannot bind me, Love,
  — Ah no! — yet I could stay

Maybe, with wings forever spread,
— Forever, and a day.

Josephine Preston Peabody.

THE THOUGHT OF HER

My love for thee doth take me unaware,
When most with lesser things my brain is wrought,
As in some nimble interchange of thought
The silence enters, and the talkers stare.
Suddenly I am still and thou art there,
A viewless visitant and unbesought,
And all my thinking trembles into nought
And all my being opens like a prayer.
Thou art the lifted Chalice in my soul,
And I a dim church at the thought of thee;
Brief be the moment, but the mass is said,
The benediction like an aureole
Is on my spirit, and shuddering through me
A rapture like the rapture of the dead.

Richard Hovey.

SONG

If love were but a little thing —
Strange love, which, more than all, is great —
One might not such devotion bring,
Early to serve and late.

If love were but a passing breath —
Wild love — which, as God knows, is sweet —
One might not make of life and death
A pillow for love's feet.

Florence Earle Coates.

THE ROSARY

THE hours I spent with thee, dear heart,
  Are as a string of pearls to me;
I count them over, every one apart,
    My rosary.

Each hour a pearl, each pearl a prayer,
  To still a heart in absence wrung;
I tell each bead unto the end — and there
    A cross is hung.

Oh, memories that bless — and burn!
  Oh, barren gain — and bitter loss!
I kiss each bead, and strive at last to learn
    To kiss the cross,
      Sweetheart,
    To kiss the cross.

Robert Cameron Rogers.

ONCE

THAT day her eyes were deep as night.
She had the motion of the rose,
The bird that veers across the light,
The waterfall that leaps and throws
Its irised spindrift to the sun.
She seemed a wind of music passing on.

Alone I saw her that one day
Stand in the window of my life.
Her sudden hand melted away
Under my lips, and without strife

I held her in my arms awhile
And drew into my lips her living smile, —

Now many a day ago and year!
Since when I dream and lie awake
In summer nights to feel her near,
And from the heavy darkness break
Glitters, till all my spirit swims
And her hand hovers on my shaking limbs.

If once again before I die
I drank the laughter of her mouth
And quenched my fever utterly,
I say, and should it cost my youth,
'T were well! for I no more should wait
Hammering midnight on the doors of fate.

Trumbull Stickney.

LOVE KNOCKS AT THE DOOR

In the pain, in the loneliness of love,
  To the heart of my sweet I fled.
I knocked at the door of her living heart,
  "Let in — let in —" I said.

"What seek you here?" the voices cried,
  "You seeker among the dead" —
"Herself I seek, herself I seek,
  Let in — let in!" I said.

They opened the door of her living heart,
  But the core thereof was dead.

They opened the core of her living heart —
  A worm at the core there fed.

"Where is my sweet, where is my sweet?"
  "She is gone away, she is fled.
Long years ago she fled away,
  She will never return," they said.

John Hall Wheelock.

THE CANDLE AND THE FLAME

THY hands are like cool herbs that bring
  Balm to men's hearts, upon them laid;
  Thy lovely-petalled lips are made
As any blossom of the spring.
But in thine eyes there is a thing,
  O Love, that makes me half afraid.

For they are old, those eyes . . . They gleam
Between the waking and the dream
  With antique wisdom, like a bright
Lamp strangled by the temple's veil,
  That beckons to the acolyte
Who prays with trembling lips and pale
  In the long watches of the night.

They are as old as Life. They were
  When proud Gomorrah reared its head
A new-born city. They were there
  When in the places of the dead
Men swathed the body of the Lord.
  They visioned Pa-wak raise the wall

Of China. They saw Carthage fall
And marked the grim Hun lead his horde.

There is no secret anywhere
Nor any joy or shame that lies
Not writ somehow in those child-eyes
Of thine, O Love, in some strange wise.
Thou art the lad Endymion,
And that great queen with spice and myrrh
From Araby, whom Solomon
Delighted, and the lust of her.

The legions marching from the sea
With Cæsar's cohorts sang of thee,
How thy fair head was more to him
Than all the land of Italy.
Yea, in the old days thou wast she
Who lured Mark Antony from home
To death and Egypt, seeing he
Lost love when he lost Rome.

Thou saw'st old Tubal strike the lyre,
Yea, first for thee the poet hurled
Defiance at God's starry choir!
Thou art the romance and the fire,
Thou art the pageant and the strife,
The clamour, mounting high and higher,
From all the lovers in the world
To all the lords of love and life.

. . . .

Perhaps the passions of mankind
Are but the torches mystical

Lit by some spirit-hand to find
The dwelling of the Master-Mind
  That knows the secret of it all,
In the great darkness and the wind.

We are the Candle, Love the Flame,
  Each little life-light flickers out,
Love bides, immortally the same:
When of life's fever we shall tire
He will desert us and the fire
  Rekindle new in prince or lout.

Twin-born of knowledge and of lust,
  He was before us, he shall be
Indifferent still of thee and me,
When shattered is life's golden cup,
When thy young limbs are shrivelled up,
And when my heart is turned to dust.

Nay, sweet, smile not to know at last
  That thou and I, or knave, or fool,
  Are but the involitient tool
Of some world-purpose vague and vast.
No bar to passion's fury set,
  With monstrous poppies spice the wine:
  For only drunk are we divine,
And only mad shall we forget!

George Sylvester Viereck.

STAINS

THE three ghosts on the lonesome road
  Spake each to one another,
"Whence came that stain about your mouth

No lifted hand may cover?"
"From eating of forbidden fruit,
Brother, my brother."

The three ghosts on the sunless road
Spake each to one another,
"Whence came that red burn on your foot
No dust nor ash may cover?"
"I stamped a neighbor's hearth-flame out,
Brother, my brother."

The three ghosts on the windless road
Spake each to one another,
"Whence came that blood upon your hand
No other hand may cover?"
"From breaking of a woman's heart,
Brother, my brother."

"Yet on the earth clean men we walked,
Glutton and Thief and Lover;
White flesh and fair it hid our stains
That no man might discover."
"Naked the soul goes up to God,
Brother, my brother."

Theodosia Garrison

DE MASSA OB DE SHEEPFOL'

De massa ob de sheepfol'
Dat guard de sheepfol' bin,
Look out in de gloomerin' meadows
Whar de long night rain begin —

So he call to de hirelin' shephe'd:
"Is my sheep — is dey all come in?"

Oh den, says de hirelin' shephe'd,
"Dey's some, dey's black and thin,
And some, dey's po' ol' wedda's —
But de res', dey's all brung in.
But de res', dey's all brung in."

Den de massa ob de sheepfol'
Dat guard de sheepfol' bin,
Goes down in de gloomerin' meadows
Whar de long night rain begin —
So he le' down de ba's ob de sheepfol',
Callin' sof': "Come in! Come in!"
Callin' sof': "Come in! Come in!"

Den up t'ro de gloomerin' meadows,
T'ro de col' night rain an' win',
An' up t'ro de gloomerin' rain-paf
Whar de sleet fa' piercin' thin —
De po' los' sheep ob de sheepfol'
Dey all comes gadderin' in.
De po' los' sheep ob de sheepfol',
Dey all comes gadderin' in!

Sarah Pratt McLean Greene.

BLACK SHEEP

FROM their folded mates they wander far,
Their ways seem harsh and wild;
They follow the beck of a baleful star,
Their paths are dream-beguiled.

Yet haply they sought but a wider range,
  Some loftier mountain-slope,
And little recked of the country strange
  Beyond the gates of hope.

And haply a bell with a luring call
  Summoned their feet to tread
Midst the cruel rocks, where the deep pitfall
  And the lurking snare are spread.

Maybe, in spite of their tameless days
  Of outcast liberty,
They're sick at heart for the homely ways
  Where their gathered brothers be.

And oft at night, when the plains fall dark
  And the hills loom large and dim,
For the Shepherd's voice they mutely hark,
  And their souls go out to him.

Meanwhile, "Black sheep! Black sheep!" we cry,
  Safe in the inner fold;
And maybe they hear, and wonder why,
  And marvel, out in the cold.

Richard Burton.

LET ME NO MORE A MENDICANT

Let me no more a mendicant
Without the gate
Of the world's kingly palace wait;
Morning is spent,

The sentinels change and challenge in the tower,
Now slant the shadows eastward hour by hour.

Open the door, O Seneschal! Within
I see them sit,
The feasters, daring destiny with wit,
Casting to win
Or lose their utmost, and men hurry by
At offices of confluent energy.

Let me not here a mendicant
Without the gate
Linger from dayspring till the night is late,
And there are sent
All homeless stars to loiter in the sky,
And beggared midnight winds to wander by.

Arthur Colton.

LINCOLN, THE MAN OF THE PEOPLE

When the Norn Mother saw the Whirlwind Hour
Greatening and darkening as it hurried on,
She left the Heaven of Heroes and came down
To make a man to meet the mortal need.
She took the tried clay of the common road —
Clay warm yet with the genial heat of Earth,
Dashed through it all a strain of prophecy;
Tempered the heap with thrill of human tears;
Then mixed a laughter with the serious stuff.
Into the shape she breathed a flame to light
That tender, tragic, ever-changing face.
Here was a man to hold against the world,
A man to match the mountains and the sea.

The color of the ground was in him, the red earth;
The smack and tang of elemental things;
The rectitude and patience of the cliff;
The good-will of the rain that loves all leaves;
The friendly welcome of the wayside well;
The courage of the bird that dares the sea;
The gladness of the wind that shakes the corn;
The pity of the snow that hides all scars;
The secrecy of streams that make their way
Beneath the mountain to the rifted rock;
The tolerance and equity of light
That gives as freely to the shrinking flower
As to the great oak flaring to the wind —
To the grave's low hill as to the Matterhorn
That shoulders out the sky.

Sprung from the West,
The strength of virgin forests braced his mind,
The hush of spacious prairies stilled his soul.
Up from log cabin to the Capitol,
One fire was on his spirit, one resolve —
To send the keen ax to the root of wrong,
Clearing a free way for the feet of God.
And evermore he burned to do his deed
With the fine stroke and gesture of a king:
He built the rail-pile as he built the State,
Pouring his splendid strength through every blow,
The conscience of him testing every stroke,
To make his deed the measure of a man.

So came the Captain with the mighty heart;
And when the judgment thunders split the house,
Wrenching the rafters from their ancient rest,

He held the ridgepole up, and spiked again
The rafters of the Home. He held his place —
Held the long purpose like a growing tree —
Held on through blame and faltered not at praise.
And when he fell in whirlwind, he went down
As when a lordly cedar, green with boughs,
Goes down with a great shout upon the hills,
And leaves a lonesome place against the sky.

Edwin Markham

THE MASTER

(Lincoln)

A FLYING word from here and there
Had sown the name at which we sneered,
But soon the name was everywhere,
To be reviled and then revered:
A presence to be loved and feared,
We cannot hide it, or deny
That we, the gentlemen who jeered,
May be forgotten by and by.

He came when days were perilous
And hearts of men were sore beguiled;
And having made his note of us,
He pondered and was reconciled.
Was ever master yet so mild
As he, and so untamable?
We doubted, even when he smiled,
Not knowing what he knew so well.

He knew that undeceiving fate
Would shame us whom he served unsought;

He knew that he must wince and wait —
The jest of those for whom he fought;
He knew devoutly what he thought
Of us and of our ridicule;
He knew that we must all be taught
Like little children in a school.

We gave a glamour to the task
That he encountered and saw through,
But little of us did he ask,
And little did we ever do.
And what appears if we review
The season when we railed and chaffed?
It is the face of one who knew
That we were learning while we laughed.

The face that in our vision feels
Again the venom that we flung,
Transfigured to the world reveals
The vigilance to which we clung.
Shrewd, hallowed, harassed, and among
The mysteries that are untold,
The face we see was never young,
Nor could it ever have been old.

For he, to whom we have applied
Our shopman's test of age and worth,
Was elemental when he died,
As he was ancient at his birth:
The saddest among kings of earth,
Bowed with a galling crown, this man
Met rancor with a cryptic mirth,
Laconic — and Olympian.

The love, the grandeur, and the fame
Are bounded by the world alone;
The calm, the smouldering, and the flame
Of awful patience were his own:
With him they are forever flown
Past all our fond self-shadowings,
Wherewith we cumber the Unknown
As with inept Icarian wings.

For we were not as other men:
'T was ours to soar and his to see.
But we are coming down again,
And we shall come down pleasantly;
Nor shall we longer disagree
On what it is to be sublime,
But flourish in our perigee
And have one Titan at a time.

Edwin Arlington Robinson.

ON THE BUILDING OF SPRINGFIELD

Let not our town be large — remembering
That little Athens was the Muses' home;
That Oxford rules the heart of London still,
That Florence gave the Renaissance to Rome.

Record it for the grandson of your son —
A city is not builded in a day:
Our little town cannot complete her soul
Till countless generations pass away.

Now let each child be joined as to a church
To her perpetual hopes, each man ordained;

Let every street be made a reverent aisle
  Where music grows, and beauty is unchained.

Let Science and Machinery and Trade
  Be slaves of her, and make her all in all —
Building against our blatant restless time
  An unseen, skillful, mediæval wall.

Let every citizen be rich toward God.
  Let Christ, the beggar, teach divinity —
Let no man rule who holds his money dear.
  Let this, our city, be our luxury.

We should build parks that students from afar
  Would choose to starve in, rather than go home —
Fair little squares, with Phidian ornament —
  Food for the spirit, milk and honeycomb.

Songs shall be sung by us in that good day —
  Songs we have written — blood within the rhyme
Beating, as when old England still was glad,
  The purple, rich, Elizabethan time.

Say, is my prophecy too fair and far?
  I only know, unless her faith be high,
The soul of this our Nineveh is doomed,
  Our little Babylon will surely die.

Some city on the breast of Illinois
  No wiser and no better at the start,
By faith shall rise redeemed — by faith shall rise
  Bearing the western glory in her heart —

The genius of the Maple, Elm and Oak,
  The secret hidden in each grain of corn —

The glory that the prairie angels sing
  At night when sons of Life and Love are born —

Born but to struggle, squalid and alone,
  Broken and wandering in their early years.
When will they make our dusty streets their goal,
  Within our attics hide their sacred tears?

When will they start our vulgar blood athrill
  With living language — words that set us free?
When will they make a path of beauty clear
  Between our riches and our liberty?

We must have many Lincoln-hearted men —
  A city is not builded in a day —
And they must do their work, and come and go
  While countless generations pass away.

Nicholas Vachel Lindsay.

THE POET'S TOWN

I

'Mid glad green miles of tillage
And fields where cattle graze,
A prosy little village,
You drowse away the days.

And yet — a wakeful glory
Clings round you as you doze;
One living lyric story
Makes music of your prose.

Here once, returning never,
The feet of song have trod;
And flashed — Oh, once forever! —
The singing Flame of God.

II

These were his fields Elysian:
With mystic eyes he saw
The sowers planting vision,
The reapers gleaning awe.

Serfs to a sordid duty,
He saw them with his heart,
Priests of the Ultimate Beauty,
Feeding the flame of art.

The weird, untempled Makers
Pulsed in the things he saw;
The wheat through its virile acres
Billowed the Song of Law.

The epic roll of the furrow
Flung from the writing plow,
The dactyl phrase of the green-rowed maize
Measured the music of Now.

III

Sipper of ancient flagons,
Often the lonesome boy
Saw in the farmers' wagons
The chariots hurled at Troy.

Trundling in dust and thunder
They rumbled up and down,

Laden with princely plunder,
Loot of the tragic Town.

And once when the rich man's daughter
Smiled on the boy at play,
Sword-storms, giddy with slaughter,
Swept back the ancient day!

War steeds shrieked in the quiet,
Far and hoarse were the cries;
And Oh, through the din and the riot,
The music of Helen's eyes!

Stabbed with the olden Sorrow,
He slunk away from the play,
For the Past and the vast To-morrow
Were wedded in his To-day.

IV

Rich with the dreamer's pillage,
An idle and worthless lad,
Least in a prosy village,
And prince in Allahabad;

Lover of golden apples,
Munching a daily crust;
Haunter of dream-built chapels,
Worshipping in the dust;

Dull to the worldly duty,
Less to the town he grew,
And more to the God of Beauty
Than even the grocer knew!

V

Corn for the buyers, and cattle —
But what could the dreamer sell?
Echoes of cloudy battle?
Music from heaven and hell?

Spices and bales of plunder
Argosied over the sea?
Tapestry woven of wonder,
And myrrh from Araby?

None of your dream-stuffs, Fellow,
Looter of Samarcand!
Gold is heavy and yellow,
And value is weighed in the hand!

VI

And yet, when the years had humbled
The Kings in the Realm of the Boy,
Song-built bastions crumbled,
Ash-heaps smothering Troy;

Thirsting for shattered flagons,
Quaffing a brackish cup,
With all of his chariots, wagons —
He never could quite grow up.

The debt to the ogre, To-morrow,
He never could comprehend:
Why should the borrowers borrow?
Why should the lenders lend?

Never an oak tree borrowed,
But took for its needs — and gave.

Never an oak tree sorrowed;
Debt was the mark of the slave.

Grass in the priceless weather
Sucked from the paps of the Earth,
And the hills that were lean it fleshed with green —
Oh, what is a lesson worth?

But still did the buyers barter
And the sellers squint at the scales;
And price was the stake of the martyr,
And cost was the lock of the jails.

VII

Windflowers herald the Maytide,
Rendering worth for worth;
Ragweeds gladden the wayside,
Biting the dugs of the Earth;

Violets, scattering glories,
Feed from the dewy gem:
But dreamers are fed by the living and dead —
And what is the gift from them?

VIII

Never a stalk of the Summer
Dreams of its mission and doom:
Only to hasten the Comer —
Martyrdom unto the Bloom.

Ever the Mighty Chooser
Plucks when the fruit is ripe,
Scorning the mass and letting it pass,
Keen for the cryptic type.

Greece in her growing season
Troubled the lands and seas,
Plotted and fought and suffered and wrought —
Building a Sophocles!

Only a faultless temple
Stands for the vassal's groan;
The harlot's strife and the faith of the wife
Blend in a graven stone.

Ne'er do the stern gods cherish
The hope of the million lives;
Always the Fact shall perish
And only the Truth survives.

Gardens of roses wither,
Shaping the perfect rose:
And the poet's song shall live for the long,
Dumb, aching years of prose.

IX

King of a Realm of Magic,
He was the fool of the town,
Hiding the ache of the tragic
Under the grin of the clown.

Worn with the vain endeavor
To fit in the sordid plan;
Doomed to be poet forever,
He longed to be only a man;

To be freed from the god's enthralling,
Back with the reeds of the stream;
Deaf to the Vision calling,
And dead to the lash of the Dream.

X

But still did the Mighty Makers
Stir in the common sod;
The corn through its awful acres
Trembled and thrilled with God!

More than a man was the sower,
Lured by a man's desire,
For a triune Bride walked close at his side —
Dew and Dust and Fire!

More than a man was the plowman,
Shouting his gee and haw;
For a something dim kept pace with him,
And ever the poet saw;

Till the winds of the cosmic struggle
Made of his flesh a flute,
To echo the tune of a whirlwind rune
Unto the million mute.

XI

Son of the Mother of mothers,
The womb and the tomb of Life,
With Fire and Air for brothers
And a clinging Dream for a wife;

Ever the soul of the dreamer
Strove with its mortal mesh,
And the lean flame grew till it fretted through
The last thin links of flesh.

Oh, rending the veil asunder,
He fled to mingle again

With the dred Orestean thunder,
The Lear of the driven rain!

XII

Once in a cycle the comet
Doubles its lonesome track.
Enriched with the tears of a thousand years,
Æschylus wanders back.

Ever inweaving, returning,
The near grows out of the far;
And Homer shall sing once more in a swing
Of the austere Polar Star.

Then what of the lonesome dreamer
With the lean blue flame in his breast?
And who was your clown for a day, O Town,
The strange, unbidden guest?

XIII

'Mid glad green miles of tillage
And fields where cattle graze;
A prosy little village,
You drowse away the days.

And yet — a wakeful glory
Clings round you as you doze;
One living, lyric story
Makes music of your prose!

John G. Neihardt.

THE NEW LIFE

Perhaps they laughed at Dante in his youth,
Told him that truth
Had unappealably been said
In the great masterpieces of the dead: —
Perhaps he listened and but bowed his head
In acquiescent honour, while his heart
Held natal tidings, — that a new life is the part
Of every man that's born,
A new life never lived before,
And a new expectant art;
It is the variations of the morn
That are forever, more and more,
The single dawning of the single truth.
So answers Dante to the heart of youth!

Witter Bynner.

MARTIN

When I am tired of earnest men,
  Intense and keen and sharp and clever,
Pursuing fame with brush or pen
  Or counting metal disks forever,
Then from the halls of shadowland
  Beyond the trackless purple sea
Old Martin's ghost comes back to stand
  Beside my desk and talk to me.

Still on his delicate pale face
  A quizzical thin smile is showing,
His cheeks are wrinkled like fine lace,
  His kind blue eyes are gay and glowing.

He wears a brilliant-hued cravat,
  A suit to match his soft gray hair,
A rakish stick, a knowing hat,
  A manner blithe and debonair.

How good, that he who always knew
  That being lovely was a duty,
Should have gold halls to wander through
  And should himself inhabit beauty.
How like his old unselfish way
  To leave those halls of splendid mirth
And comfort those condemned to stay
  Upon the bleak and sombre earth.

Some people ask: What cruel chance
  Made Martin's life so sad a story?
Martin? Why, he exhaled romance
  And wore an overcoat of glory.
A fleck of sunlight in the street,
  A horse, a book, a girl who smiled,—
Such visions made each moment sweet
  For this receptive, ancient child.

Because it was old Martin's lot
  To be, not make, a decoration,
Shall we then scorn him, having not
  His genius of appreciation?
Rich joy and love he got and gave;
  His heart was merry as his dress.
Pile laurel wreaths upon his grave
  Who did not gain, but was, success.

Joyce Kilmer.

"AS IN THE MIDST OF BATTLE THERE IS ROOM"

As in the midst of battle there is room
  For thoughts of love, and in foul sin for mirth;
  As gossips whisper of a trinket's worth
Spied by the death-bed's flickering candle-gloom;
As in the crevices of Cæsar's tomb
  The sweet herbs flourish on a little earth:
  So in this great disaster of our birth
We can be happy, and forget our doom.

For morning, with a ray of tenderest joy
  Gilding the iron heaven, hides the truth,
And evening gently woos us to employ
  Our grief in idle catches. Such is youth;
Till from that summer's trance we wake, to find
Despair before us, vanity behind.

George Santayana.

EX LIBRIS

In an old book at even as I read
  Fast fading words adown my shadowy page,
  I crossed a tale of how, in other age,
At Arqua, with his books around him, sped
The word to Petrarch; and with noble head
  Bowed gently o'er his volume that sweet sage
  To Silence paid his willing seigniorage.
And they who found him whispered, "He is dead!"

Thus timely from old comradeships would I
  To Silence also rise. Let there be night,

Stillness, and only these staid watchers by,
  And no light shine save my low study light —
Lest of his kind intent some human cry
  Interpret not the Messenger aright.

Arthur Upson.

THE POET

HIMSELF is least afraid
  When the singing lips in the dust
With all mute lips are laid.
  For thither all men must.
Nor is the end long stayed.

But he, having cast his song
  Upon the faithful air
And given it speed — is strong
  That last strange hour to dare,
Nor wills to tarry long.

Adown immortal time
  That greater self shall pass,
And wear its eager prime
  And lend the youth it has
Like one far blowing chime.

He has made sure the quest
  And now — his word gone forth —
May have his perfect rest
  Low in the tender earth,
The wind across his breast.

Mildred McNeal Sweeney.

WHEN I HAVE GONE WEIRD WAYS

When I have finished with this episode,
Left the hard, uphill road,
And gone weird ways to seek another load,
  Oh, friends, regret me not, nor weep for me,
  Child of Infinity!

Nor dig a grave, nor rear for me a tomb
To say with lying writ: "Here in the gloom
He who loved bigness takes a narrow room,
  Content to pillow here his weary head,
  For he is dead."

But give my body to the funeral pyre,
And bid the laughing fire,
Eager and strong and swift, like my desire,
  Scatter my subtle essence into space,
  Free me of time and place.

And sweep the bitter ashes from the hearth,
Fling back the dust I borrowed from the earth
Into the chemic broil of death and birth,
  The vast alembic of the cryptic scheme,
  Warm with the master-dream.

And thus, O little house that sheltered me,
Dissolve again in wind and rain, to be
Part of the cosmic weird economy.
  And, Oh, how oft with new life shalt thou lift
  Out of the atom-drift!

John G. Neihardt.

TRUMBULL STICKNEY

I

In silence, solitude and stern surmise
His faith was tried and proved commensurate
With life and death. The stone-blind eyes of Fate
Perpetually stared into his eyes,
Yet to the hazard of the enterprise
He brought his soul, expectant and elate,
And challenged, like a champion at the Gate,
Death's undissuadable austerities.
And thus, full-armed in all that Truth reprieves
From dissolution, he beheld the breath
Of daybreak flush his thought's exalted ways,
While, like Dodona's sad, prophetic leaves,
Round him the scant, supreme, momentous days
Trembled and murmured in the wind of Death.

II

There moved a Presence always by his side,
With eyes of pleasure and passion and wild tears,
And on her lips the murmur of many years,
And in her hair the chaplets of a bride;
And with him, hour by hour, came one beside,
Scatheless of Time and Time's vicissitude,
Whose lips, perforce of endless solitude,
Were silent and whose eyes were blind and wide.
But when he died came One who wore a wreath
Of star-light, and with fingers calm and bland
Smoothed from his brows the trace of mortal pain;
And of the two who stood on either hand,
"This one is Life," he said, "And this is Death,
And I am Love and Lord over these twain!"

George Cabot Lodge.

SENTENCE

SHALL I say that what heaven gave
  Earth has taken? —
Or that sleepers in the grave
  Reawaken?

One sole sentence can I know,
  Can I say:
You, my comrade, had to go,
  I to stay.

Witter Bynner.

COMRADES

WHERE are the friends that I knew in my Maying,
  In the days of my youth, in the first of my roaming?
We were dear; we were leal; O, far we went straying;
  Now never a heart to my heart comes homing! —
Where is he now, the dark boy slender
  Who taught me bare-back, stirrup and reins?
I loved him; he loved me; my beautiful, tender
  Tamer of horses on grass-grown plains.

Where is he now whose eyes swam brighter,
  Softer than love, in his turbulent charms;
Who taught me to strike, and to fall, dear fighter,
  And gathered me up in his boyhood arms;
Taught me the rifle, and with me went riding,
  Suppled my limbs to the horseman's war;
Where is he now, for whom my heart's biding,
  Biding, biding — but he rides far!

O love that passes the love of woman!
  Who that hath felt it shall ever forget,
When the breath of life with a throb turns human,
  And a lad's heart is to a lad's heart set?
Ever, forever, lover and rover —
  They shall cling, nor each from other shall part
Till the reign of the stars in the heavens be over,
  And life is dust in each faithful heart!

They are dead, the American grasses under;
  There is no one now who presses my side;
By the African chotts I am riding asunder,
  And with great joy ride I the last great ride.
I am fey; I am fain of sudden dying;
  Thousands of miles there is no one near;
And my heart — all the night it is crying, crying
  In the bosoms of dead lads darling-dear.

Hearts of my music — them dark earth covers;
  Comrades to die, and to die for, were they;
In the width of the world there were no such rovers —
  Back to back, breast to breast, it was ours to stay;
And the highest on earth was the vow that we cherished,
  To spur forth from the crowd and come back never more,
And to ride in the track of great souls perished
  Till the nests of the lark shall roof us o'er.

Yet lingers a horseman on Altai highlands,
  Who hath joy of me, riding the Tartar glissade;
And one, far faring o'er orient islands
  Whose blood yet glints with my blade's accolade;

North, west, east, I fling you my last hallooing,
  Last love to the breasts where my own has bled;
Through the reach of the desert my soul leaps pursuing
  My star where it rises a Star of the Dead.

George Edward Woodberry.

COMRADES

COMRADES, pour the wine to-night
For the parting is with dawn!
Oh, the clink of cups together,
With the daylight coming on!
Greet the morn
With a double horn,
When strong men drink together!

Comrades, gird your swords to-night,
For the battle is with dawn!
Oh, the clash of shields together,
With the triumph coming on!
Greet the foe,
And lay him low,
When strong men fight together!

Comrades, watch the tides to-night,
For the sailing is with dawn!
Oh, to face the spray together,
With the tempest coming on!
Greet the sea
With a shout of glee,
When strong men roam together!

Comrades, give a cheer to-night,
For the dying is with dawn!

Oh, to meet the stars together,
With the silence coming on!
Greet the end
As a friend a friend,
When strong men die together!

Richard Hovey.

CALVERLY'S

We go no more to Calverly's,
For there the lights are few and low;
And who are there to see by them,
Or what they see, we do not know.
Poor strangers of another tongue
May now creep in from anywhere,
And we, forgotten, be no more
Than twilight on a ruin there.

We two, the remnant. All the rest
Are cold and quiet. You nor I,
Nor fiddle now, nor flagon-lid,
May ring them back from where they lie.
No fame delays oblivion
For them, but something yet survives:
A record written fair, could we
But read the book of scattered lives.

There'll be a page for Leffingwell,
And one for Lingard, the Moon-calf;
And who knows what for Clavering,
Who died because he could n't laugh?
Who knows or cares? No sign is here,
No face, no voice, no memory;

No Lingard with his eerie joy,
No Clavering, no Calverly.

We cannot have them here with us
To say where their light lives are gone,
Or if they be of other stuff
Than are the moons of Ilion.
So, be their place of one estate
With ashes, echoes, and old wars, —
Or ever we be of the night,
Or we be lost among the stars.

Edwin Arlington Robinson.

URIEL

(IN MEMORY OF WILLIAM VAUGHN MOODY)

I

URIEL, you that in the ageless sun
Sit in the awful silences of light,
Singing of vision hid from human sight, —
Prometheus, beautiful rebellious one!
And you, Deucalion,
For whose blind seed was brought the illuming spark,
Are you not gathered, now his day is done,
Beside the brink of that relentless dark —
The dark where your dear singer's ghost is gone?

II

Imagined beings, who majestic blend
Your forms with beauty! — questing, unconfined,
The mind conceived you, though the quenchèd mind
Goes down in dark where you in dawn ascend.

Our songs can but suspend
The ultimate silence: yet could song aspire
The realms of mortal music to extend
And wake a Sibyl's voice or Seraph's lyre —
How should it tell the dearness of a friend?

III

The simplest is the inexpressible;
The heart of music still evades the Muse,
And arts of men the heart of man suffuse,
And saddest things are made of silence still.
In vain the senses thrill
To give our sorrows glorious relief
In pyre of verse and pageants volatile,
And I, in vain, to speak for him my grief
Whose spirit of fire invokes my waiting will.

IV

To him the best of friendship needs must be
Uttered no more; yet was he so endowed
That Poetry because of him is proud
And he more noble for his poetry,
Wherefore infallibly
I obey the strong compulsion which this verse
Lays on my lips with strange austerity —
Now that his voice is silent — to rehearse
For my own heart how he was dear to me.

V

Not by your gradual sands, elusive Time,
We measure your gray sea, that never rests;
The bleeding hour-glasses in our breasts
Mete with quick pangs the ebbing of our prime,

And drip, like sudden rime
In March, that melts to runnels from a pane
The south breathes on — oblivion of sublime
Crystallizations, and the ruthless wane
Of glittering stars, that scarce had range to climb.

VI

Darkling those constellations of his soul
Glimmered, while racks of stellar lightning shot
The white, creative meteors of thought
Through that last night, where — clad in cloudy
stole —
Beside his ebbing shoal
Of life-blood, stood Saint Paul, blazing a theme
Of living drama from a fiery scroll
Across his stretchèd vision as in dream —
When Death, with blind dark, blotted out the whole.

VII

And yet not all: though darkly alien
Those uncompleted worlds of work to be
Are waned; still, touched by them, the memory
Gives afterglow; and now that comes again
The mellow season when
Our eyes last met, his kindling currents run
Quickening within me gladness and new ken
Of life, that I have shared his prime with one
Who wrought large-minded for the love of men.

VIII

But not alone to share that large estate
Of work and interchange of communings —
The little human paths to heavenly things

Were also ours: the casual, intimate
Vistas, which consecrate —
With laughter and quick tears — the dusty noon
Of days, and by moist beams irradiate
Our plodding minds with courage, and attune
The fellowship that bites its thumb at fate.

IX

Where art thou now, mine host Guffanti? — where
The iridescence of thy motley troop!
Ah, where the merry, animated group
That snuggled elbows for an extra chair,
When space was none to spare,
To pour the votive Chianti for a toast
To dramas dark and lyrics debonair,
The while, to *Bella Napoli*, mine host
Exhaled his Parmazan, Parnassan air!

X

Thy Parmazan, immortal laird of ease,
Can never mold, thy caviare is blest,
While still our glowing Uriel greets the rest
Around thy royal board of memories,
Where sit, the salt of these,
He of the laughter of a Hundred Lights,
Blithe Eldorado of high poesies,
And he — of enigmatic gentle knights
The kindly keen — who sings of *Calverly's*.

XI

Because he never wore his sentient heart
For crows and jays to peck, ofttimes to such
He seemed a silent fellow, who o'ermuch

Held from the general gossip-ground apart,
Or tersely spoke, and tart:
How should they guess what eagle tore, within,
His quick of sympathy for humblest smart
Of human wretchedness, or probed his spleen
Of scorn against the hypocritic mart!

XII

Sometimes insufferable seemed to come
That wrath of sympathy: One windy night
We watched through squalid panes, forlornly white, —
Amid immense machines' incessant hum —
Frail figures, gaunt and dumb,
Of overlabored girls and children, bowed
Above their slavish toil: "O God! — A bomb,
A bomb!" he cried, "and with one fiery cloud
Expunge the horrible Cæsars of this slum!"

XIII

Another night dreams on the Cornish hills:
Trembling within the low moon's pallid fires,
The tall corn-tassels lift their fragrant spires;
From filmy spheres, a liquid starlight fills —
Like dew of daffodils —
The fragile dark, where multitudinous
The rhythmic, intermittent silence thrills,
Like song, the valleys. — "Hark!" he murmurs,
"Thus
May bards from crickets learn their canticles!"

XIV

Now Morning, not less lavish of her sweets,
Leads us along the woodpaths — in whose hush

The quivering alchemy of the pure thrush
Cools from above the balsam-dripping heats —
To find, in green retreats,
'Mid men of clay, the great, quick-hearted man
Whose subtle art our human age secretes,
Or him whose brush, tinct with cerulean,
Blooms with soft castle-towers and cloud-capped
fleets.

XV

Still to the sorcery of August skies
In frillèd crimson flaunt the hollyhocks,
Where, lithely poised along the garden walks,
His little maid enamoured blithe outvies
The dipping butterflies
In motion — ah, in grace how grown the while,
Since he was wont to render to her eyes
His knightly court, or touch with flitting smile
Her father's heart by his true flatteries!

XVI

But summer's golden pastures boast no trail
So splendid as our fretted snowshoes blaze
Where, sharp across the amethystine ways,
Iron Ascutney looms in azure mail,
And, like a frozen grail,
The frore sun sets, intolerably fair;
Mute, in our homebound snow-tracks, we exhale
The silvery cold, and soon — where bright logs flare —
Talk the long indoor hours, till embers fail.

XVII

Ah, with the smoke what smouldering desires
Waft to the starlight up the swirling flue! —

Thoughts that may never, as the swallows do,
Nest circling homeward to their native fires!
Ardors the soul suspires
The extinct stars drink with the dreamer's breath;
The morning-song of Eden's early choirs
Grows dim with Adam; close at the ear of death
Relentless angels tune our earthly lyres!

XVIII

Let it be so: More sweet it is to be
A listener of love's ephemeral song,
And live with beauty though it be not long,
And die enamoured of eternity,
Though in the apogee
Of time there sit no individual
Godhead of life, than to reject the plea
Of passionate beauty: loveliness is all,
And love is more divine than memory.

Percy MacKaye.

AZRAEL

THE angels in high places
  Who minister to us,
Reflect God's smile, — their faces
  Are luminous;
Save one, whose face is hidden,
  (The Prophet saith),
The unwelcome, the unbidden,
  Azrael, Angel of Death.
And yet that veilèd face, I know
  Is lit with pitying eyes,
Like those faint stars, the first to glow
  Through cloudy winter skies.

That they may never tire,
  Angels, by God's decree,
Bear wings of snow and fire, —
  Passion and purity;
Save one, all unavailing,
  (The Prophet saith),
His wings are gray and trailing,
  Azrael, Angel of Death.
And yet the souls that Azrael brings
  Across the dark and cold,
Look up beneath those folded wings,
  And find them lined with gold.

Robert Gilbert Welsh.

THE FLIGHT

Upon a cloud among the stars we stood.
The angel raised his hand and looked and said,
"Which world, of all yon starry myriad,
Shall we make wing to?" The still solitude
Became a harp whereon his voice and mood
Made spheral music round his haloed head.
I spake — for then I had not long been dead —
"Let me look round upon the vasts, and brood
A moment on these orbs ere I decide . . .
What is yon lower star that beauteous shines
And with soft splendour now incarnadines
Our wings? — *There* would I go and there abide."
Then he as one who some child's thought divines:
"That is the world where yesternight you died."

Lloyd Mifflin.

THE RIVAL

I so loved once, when Death came by I hid
 Away my face,
And all my sweetheart's tresses she undid
 To make my hiding-place.

The dread shade passed me thus unheeding; and
 I turned me then
To calm my love — kiss down her shielding hand
 And comfort her again.

And lo! she answered not: and she did sit
 All fixedly,
With her fair face and the sweet smile of it,
 In love with Death, not me.

James Whitcomb Riley.

A RHYME OF DEATH'S INN

A RHYME of good Death's inn!
 My love came to that door;
And she had need of many things,
 The way had been so sore.

My love she lifted up her head,
 "And is there room?" said she;
"There was no room in Bethlehem's inn
 For Christ who died for me."

But said the keeper of the inn,
 "His name is on the door."

My love then straightway entered there:
  She hath come back no more.

Lizette Woodworth Reese.

THE OUTER GATE

Life said: "My house is thine with all its store:
  Behold I open shining ways to thee —
  Of every inner portal make thee free:
O child, I may not bar the outer door.
Go from me if thou wilt, to come no more;
  But all thy pain is mine, thy flesh of me;
  And must I hear thee, faint and woefully,
Call on me from the darkness and implore?"

Nay, mother, for I follow at thy will.
  But oftentimes thy voice is sharp to hear,
    Thy trailing fragrance heavy on the breath;
Always the outer hall is very still,
  And on my face a pleasant wind and clear
    Blows straitly from the narrow gate of Death.

Nora May French.

THE ASHES IN THE SEA

N. M. F.

Whither, with blue and pleading eyes, —
  Whither, with cheeks that held the light
Of winter's dawn in cloudless skies,
  Evadne, was thy flight?

Such as a sister's was thy brow;
  Thy hair seemed fallen from the moon —

Part of its radiance, as now,
  Of shifting tide and dune.

Did Autumn's grieving lure thee hence,
  Or silence ultimate beguile?
Ever our things of consequence
  Awakened but thy smile.

Is it with thee that ocean takes
  A stranger sorrow to its tone?
With thee the star of evening wakes
  More beautiful, more lone?

For wave and hill and sky betray
  A subtle tinge and touch of thee;
Thy shadow lingers in the day,
  Thy voice in winds to be.

Beauty — hast thou discovered her
  By deeper seas no moons control?
What stars have magic now to stir
  Thy swift and wilful soul?

Or may thy heart no more forget
  The grievous world that once was home,
That here, where love awaits thee yet,
  Thou seemest yet to roam?

For most, far-wandering, I guess
  Thy witchery on the haunted mind,
In valleys of thy loneliness,
  Made clean with ocean's wind.

And most thy presence here seems told,
  A waif of elemental deeps,
When, at its vigils unconsoled,
  Some night of winter weeps.

George Sterling.

"WE NEEDS MUST BE DIVIDED IN THE TOMB"

We needs must be divided in the tomb,
  For I would die among the hills of Spain,
  And o'er the treeless, melancholy plain
Await the coming of the final gloom.
But thou — O pitiful! — wilt find scant room
  Among thy kindred by the northern main,
  And fade into the drifting mist again,
The hemlocks' shadow, or the pines' perfume.

Let gallants lie beside their ladies' dust
  In one cold grave, with mortal love inurned;
Let the sea part our ashes, if it must,
  The souls fled thence which love immortal burned,
For they were wedded without bond of lust,
  And nothing of our heart to earth returned.

George Santayana.

DEPARTURE

My true love from her pillow rose
  And wandered down the summer lane.
She left her house to the wind's carouse,
  And her chamber wide to the rain.

She did not stop to don her coat,
  She did not stop to smooth her bed —
But out she went in glad content
  There where the bright path led.

She did not feel the beating storm,
  But fled like a sunbeam, white and frail,
To the sea, to the air, somewhere, somewhere —
  I have not found her trail.

Hermann Hagedorn.

SONG

She's somewhere in the sunlight strong,
  Her tears are in the falling rain,
She calls me in the wind's soft song,
  And with the flowers she comes again.

Yon bird is but her messenger,
  The moon is but her silver car;
Yea! Sun and moon are sent by her,
  And every wistful, waiting star.

Richard Le Gallienne.

THE INVISIBLE BRIDE

The low-voiced girls that go
  In gardens of the Lord,
Like flowers of the field they grow
  In sisterly accord.

Their whispering feet are white
  Along the leafy ways;

They go in whirls of light
  Too beautiful for praise.

And in their band forsooth
  Is one to set me free —
The one that touched my youth —
  The one God gave to me.

She kindles the desire
  Whereby the gods survive —
The white ideal fire
  That keeps my soul alive.

Now at the wondrous hour,
  She leaves her star supreme,
And comes in the night's still power,
  To touch me with a dream.

Sibyl of mystery
  On roads unknown to men,
Softly she comes to me,
  And goes to God again.

Edwin Markham.

THE INVERTED TORCH

THREADING a darksome passage all alone,
The taper's flame, by envious current blown,
Crouched low, and eddied round, as in affright,
So challenged by the vast and hostile night,
Then down I held the taper; — swift and fain
Up climbed the lovely flower of light again!

Thou Kindler of the spark of life divine,
Be henceforth the Inverted Torch a sign
That, though the flame beloved thou dost depress,
Thou wilt not speed it into nothingness;
But out of nether gloom wilt reinspire,
And homeward lift the keen empyreal fire!

Edith M. Thomas.

NIGHT'S MARDI GRAS

Night is the true democracy. When day
Like some great monarch with his train has passed,
In regal pomp and splendor to the last,
The stars troop forth along the Milky Way,
A jostling crowd, in radiant disarray,
On heaven's broad boulevard in pageants vast.
And things of earth, the hunted and outcast,
Come from their haunts and hiding-places; yea,
Even from the nooks and crannies of the mind
Visions uncouth and vagrant fancies start,
And specters of dead joy, that shun the light,
And impotent regrets and terrors blind,
Each one, in form grotesque, playing its part
In the fantastic Mardi Gras of Night.

Edward J. Wheeler.

THE MYSTIC

There is a quest that calls me,
In nights when I am lone,
The need to ride where the ways divide
The Known from the Unknown.

I mount what thought is near me
  And soon I reach the place,
The tenuous rim where the Seen grows dim
  And the Sightless hides its face.

I have ridden the wind,
I have ridden the sea,
I have ridden the moon and stars.
I have set my feet in the stirrup seat
Of a comet coursing Mars.
And everywhere
Thro' the earth and air
My thought speeds, lightning-shod,
It comes to a place where checking pace
It cries, "Beyond lies God!"

It calls me out of the darkness,
  It calls me out of sleep,
"Ride! ride! for you must, to the end of Dust!"
  It bids — and on I sweep
To the wide outposts of Being,
  Where there is Gulf alone —
And thro' a Vast that was never passed
  I listen for Life's tone.

I have ridden the wind,
I have ridden the night,
I have ridden the ghosts that flee
From the vaults of death like a chilling breath
Over eternity.
And everywhere
Is the world laid bare —
Ether and star and clod —

Until I wind to its brink and find
But the cry, "Beyond lies God!"

It calls me and ever calls me!
And vainly I reply,
"Fools only ride where the ways divide
What Is from the Whence and Why"!
I'm lifted into the saddle
Of thoughts too strong to tame
And down the deeps and over the steeps
I find — ever the same.

I have ridden the wind,
I have ridden the stars,
I have ridden the force that flies
With far intent thro' the firmament
And each to each allies.
And everywhere
That a thought may dare
To gallop, mine has trod —
Only to stand at last on the strand
Where just beyond lies God.

Cale Young Rice.

"I WOULD I MIGHT FORGET THAT I AM I"

I WOULD I might forget that I am I,
And break the heavy chain that binds me fast,
Whose links about myself my deeds have cast.
What in the body's tomb doth buried lie
Is boundless; 't is the spirit of the sky,
Lord of the future, guardian of the past,

And soon must forth, to know his own at last.
In his large life to live, I fain would die.

Happy the dumb beast, hungering for food,
But calling not his suffering his own;
Blessèd the angel, gazing on all good,
But knowing not he sits upon a throne;
Wretched the mortal, pondering his mood,
And doomed to know his aching heart alone.

George Santayana.

TO WILLIAM SHARP

(*Fiona Macleod*)

The waves about Iona dirge,
The wild winds trumpet over Skye;
Shrill around Arran's cliff-bound verge
The gray gulls cry.

Spring wraps its transient scarf of green,
Its heathery robe, round slope and scar;
And night, the scudding wrack between,
Lights its lone star.

But you who loved these outland isles,
Their gleams, their glooms, their mysteries,
Their eldritch lures, their druid wiles,
Their tragic seas,

Will heed no more, in mortal guise,
The potent witchery of their call,
If dawn be regnant in the skies,
Or evenfall.

Yet, though where suns Sicilian beam
  The loving earth enfolds your form,
I can but deem these coasts of dream
  And hovering storm

Still thrall your spirit — that it bides
  By far Iona's kelp-strewn shore,
There lingering till time and tides
  Shall surge no more.

Clinton Scollard.

THE QUIET SINGER

(*Ave! Francis Thompson*)

He had been singing — but I had not heard his voice;
He had been weaving lovely dreams of song,
O many a morning long.
But I, remote and far,
Under an alien star,
Listened to other singers, other birds,
And other silver words.
But does the skylark, singing sweet and clear,
Beg the cold world to hear?
Rather he sings for very rapture of singing,
At dawn, or in the blue, mild Summer noon,
Knowing that, late or soon,
His wealth of beauty, and his high notes, ringing
Above the earth, will make some heart rejoice.
He sings, albeit alone,
Spendthrift of each pure tone,
Hoarding no single song,
No cadence wild and strong.
But one day, from a friend far overseas,

As if upon the breeze,
There came the teeming wonder of his words —
A golden troop of birds,
Caged in a little volume made to love;
Singing, singing,
Flinging, flinging
Their breaking hearts on mine, and swiftly bringing
Tears, and the peace thereof.
How the world woke anew!
How the days broke anew!
Before my tear-blind eyes a tapestry
I seemed to see,
Woven of all the dreams dead or to be.
Hills, hills of song, Springs of eternal bloom,
Autumns of golden pomp and purple gloom
Were hung upon his loom.
Winters of pain, roses with awful thorns,
Yet wondrous faith in God's dew-drenchèd morns —
These, all these I saw,
With that ecstatic awe
Wherewith one looks into Eternity.

And then I knew that, though I had not heard
His voice before,
His quiet singing, like some quiet bird
At some one's distant door,
Had made my own more sweet; had made it more
Lovely, in one of God's miraculous ways.
I knew then why the days
Had seemed to me more perfect when the Spring
Came with old bourgeoning;
For somewhere in the world his voice was raised,
And somewhere in the world his heart was breaking;

And never a flower but knew it, sweetly taking
Beauty more high and noble for his sake,
As a whole wood grows lovelier for the wail
Of one sad nightingale.

Yet if the Springs long past
Seemed wonderful before I heard his voice,
I tremble at the beauty I shall see
In seasons still to be,
Now that his songs are mine while Life shall last.
O now for me
New floods of vision open suddenly . . .
Rejoice, my heart! Rejoice
That you have heard the Quiet Singer's voice!

Charles Hanson Towne.

AFTER A DOLMETSCH CONCERT

Out of the conquered Past
  Unravishable Beauty;
Hearts that are dew and dust
  Rebuking the dream of Death;
Flower o' the clay downcast
  Triumphant in Earth's aroma;
Strings that were strained in rust
  A-tremble with Music's breath!

Wine that was spilt in haste
  Arising in fumes more precious;
Garlands that fell forgot
  Rooting to wondrous bloom;
Youth that would flow to waste
  Pausing in pool-green valleys —

And Passion that lasted not
  Surviving the voiceless Tomb!

Arthur Upson.

ON A FLY-LEAF OF BURNS' SONGS

These are the best of him,
Pathos and jest of him;
Earth holds the rest of him.

Passions were strong in him, —
Pardon the wrong in him;
Hark to the song in him! —

Each little lyrical
Grave or satirical
Musical miracle!

Frederic Lawrence Knowles.

MINIVER CHEEVY

Miniver Cheevy, child of scorn,
  Grew lean while he assailed the seasons;
He wept that he was ever born,
  And he had reasons.

Miniver loved the days of old
  When swords were bright and steeds were prancing;
The vision of a warrior bold
  Would set him dancing.

Miniver sighed for what was not,
  And dreamed, and rested from his labors;

He dreamed of Thebes and Camelot,
  And Priam's neighbors.

Miniver mourned the ripe renown
  That made so many a name so fragrant;
He mourned Romance, now on the town,
  And Art, a vagrant.

Miniver loved the Medici,
  Albeit he had never seen one;
He would have sinned incessantly
  Could he have been one.

Miniver cursed the commonplace
  And eyed a khaki suit with loathing;
He missed the mediæval grace
  Of iron clothing.

Miniver scorned the gold he sought,
  But sore annoyed was he without it;
Miniver thought, and thought, and thought,
  And thought about it.

Miniver Cheevy, born too late,
  Scratched his head and kept on thinking;
Miniver coughed, and called it fate,
  And kept on drinking.

Edwin Arlington Robinson.

AT THE END OF THE DAY

THERE is no escape by the river,
There is no flight left by the fen;

We are compassed about by the shiver
Of the night of their marching men.
Give a cheer!
For our hearts shall not give way.
Here's to a dark to-morrow,
And here's to a brave to-day!

The tale of their hosts is countless,
And the tale of ours a score;
But the palm is naught to the dauntless,
And the cause is more and more.
Give a cheer!
We may die, but not give way.
Here's to a silent morrow,
And here's to a stout to-day!

God has said: "Ye shall fail and perish;
But the thrill ye have felt to-night
I shall keep in my heart and cherish
When the worlds have passed in night."
Give a cheer!
For the soul shall not give way.
Here's to the greater to-morrow
That is born of a great to-day!

Now shame on the craven truckler
And the puling things that mope!
We've a rapture for our buckler
That outwears the wings of hope.
Give a cheer!
For our joy shall not give way.
Here's in the teeth of to-morrow
To the glory of to-day!

Richard Hovey.

THE JOY OF THE HILLS

I RIDE on the mountain tops, I ride;
I have found my life and am satisfied.
Onward I ride in the blowing oats,
Checking the field-lark's rippling notes —
        Lightly I sweep
        From steep to steep:
Over my head through the branches high
Come glimpses of a rushing sky;
The tall oats brush my horse's flanks;
Wild poppies crowd on the sunny banks;
A bee booms out of the scented grass;
A jay laughs with me as I pass.

I ride on the hills, I forgive, I forget
        Life's hoard of regret —
        All the terror and pain
        Of the chafing chain.
        Grind on, O cities, grind:
        I leave you a blur behind.
I am lifted elate — the skies expand:
Here the world's heaped gold is a pile of sand.
Let them weary and work in their narrow walls:
I ride with the voices of waterfalls!

I swing on as one in a dream — I swing
Down the airy hollows, I shout, I sing!
The world is gone like an empty word:
My body's a bough in the wind, my heart a bird!

Edwin Markham.

THE LESSER CHILDREN

A THRENODY AT THE HUNTING SEASON

In the middle of August when the southwest wind
Blows after sunset through the leisuring air,
And on the sky nightly the mythic hind
Leads down the sullen dog star to his lair,
After the feverous vigil of July,
When the loud pageant of the year's high noon
Passed up the ways of time to sing and part,
Grief also wandered by
From out the lovers and the leaves of June,
And by the wizard spices of his hair
I knew his heart was very Love's own heart.
Deep within dreams he led me out of doors
As from the upper vault the night outpours,
And when I saw that to him all the skies
Yearned as a sea asleep yearns to its shores,
He took a little clay and touched my eyes.

What saw I then, what heard?
Multitudes, multitudes, under the moon they stirred!
The weaker brothers of our earthly breed;
Watchmen of whom our safety takes no heed;
Swift helpers of the wind that sowed the seed
Before the first field was or any fruit;
Warriors against the bivouac of the weed;
Earth's earliest ploughmen for the tender root,
All came about my head and at my feet
A thousand, thousand sweet,
With starry eyes not even raised to plead;
Bewildered, driven, hiding, fluttering, mute!

And I beheld and saw them one by one
Pass and become as nothing in the night.
Clothed on with red they were who once were white;
Drooping, who once led armies to the sun,
Of whom the lowly grass now topped the flight:
In scarlet faint, who once were brave in brown;
Climbers and builders of the silent town,
Creepers and burrowers all in crimson dye,
Winged mysteries of song that from the sky
Once dashed long music down.

O who would take away music from the earth?
Have we so much? Or love upon the hearth?
No more — they faded;
The great trees bending between birth and birth
Sighed for them, and the night wind's hoarse rebuff
Shouted the shame of which I was persuaded.
Shall Nature's only pausing be by men invaded?
Or shall we lay grief's fagots on her shoulders bare?
Has she not borne enough?
Soon will the mirroring woodland pools begin to con
her,
And her sad immemorial passion come upon her;
Lo, would you add despair unto despair?
Shall not the Spring be answer to her prayer?
Must her uncomforted heavens overhead,
Weeping, look down on tears and still behold
Only wings broken or a fledgling dead,
Or underfoot the meadows that wore gold
Die, and the leaves go mourning to the mould
Beneath poor dead and desperate feet
Of folk who in next summer's meadows shall not meet?

Who has not seen in the high gulf of light
What, lower, was a bird, but now
Is moored and altered quite
Into an island of unshaded joy?
To whom the mate below upon the bough
Shouts once and brings him from his high employ.
Yet speeding he forgot not of the cloud
Where he from glory sprang and burned aloud,
But took a little of the day,
A little of the colored sky,
And of the joy that would not stay
He wove a song that cannot die.
Then, then — the unfathomable shame;
The one last wrong arose from out the flame,
The ravening hate that hated not was hurled
Bidding the radiant love once more beware,
Bringing one more loneliness on the world,
And one more blindness in the unseen air.
Nor may the smooth regret, the pitying oath
Shed on such utter bitter any leaven.
Only the pleading flowers that knew them both
Hold all their bloody petals up to heaven.

Winds of the fall that all year to and fro
Somewhere upon the earth go wandering,
You saw, you moaned, you know:
Withhold not then unto all time to tell
Lest unborn others of us see this thing.
Bring our sleek, comfortable reason low:
Recount how souls grown tremulous as a bell
Came forth each other and the day to greet
In morning air all Indian-Summer sweet,
And crept upstream, through wood or field or brake,

Most tremblingly to take
What crumbs that from the Master's table fell.
Cry with what thronging thunders they were met,
And hide not how the least leaf was made wet.
Cry till no watcher says that all is well
With raucous discord through the leaning spheres.
But tell
With tears, with tears
How the last man is harmed even as they
Who on these dawns are fire, at dusk are clay.
Record the dumb and wise,
No less than those who lived in singing guise,
Whose choric hearts lit each wild green arcade.
Make men to see their eyes,
Forced to suspect behind each reed or rose
The thorn of lurking foes.
And O, before the daylight goes,
After the deed against the skies,
After the last belief and longing dies,
Make men again to see their eyes
Whose piteous casements now all unafraid
Peer out to that far verge where evermore,
Beyond all woe for which a tear atones,
The likeness of our own dishonor moans,
A sea that has no bottom and no shore.

What shall be done
By you, shy folk who cease thus heart by heart?
You for whose fate such fate forever hovers?
O little lovers,
If you would still have nests beneath the sun
Gather your broods about you and depart,
Before the stony forward-pressing faces

Into the lands bereft of any sound;
The solemn and compassionate desert places.
Give unto men no more the strong delight
To know that underneath the frozen ground
Dwells the warm life and all the quick, pure lore.
Take from our eyes the glory of great flight.
Let us behold no more
People untroubled by a Fate's veiled eyes,
Leave us upon an earth of faith forlorn.
No more wild tidings from the sweet far skies
Of love's long utmost heavenward endeavor.
So shall the silence pour on us forever
The streaming arrows of unutterable scorn.

Nor shall the cry of famine be a shield
The altar of a brutish mood to hide.
Stains, stains, upon the lintels of our doors
Wail to be justified.
Shall there be mutterings at the seasons' yield?
Has eye of man seen bared the granary floors?
Are the fields wasted? Spilled the oil and wine?
Is the fat seed under the clod decayed?
Does ever the fig tree languish or the vine?
Who has beheld the harvest promise fade ?
Or any orchard heavy with fruit asway
Withered away?
No, not these things, but grosser things than these
Are the dim parents of a guilt not dim;
Ancestral urges out of old caves blowing,
When Fear watched at our coming and our going
The horror of the chattering face of Whim.
Hates, cruelties new fallen from the trees
Whereto we clung with impulse sad for love,

Shames we have had all time to rid us of,
Disgraces cold and sorrows long bewept,
Recalled, revived, and kept,
Unmeaning quarrels, blood-compelling lust,
And snarling woes from our old home, the dust.

Yet even of these one saving shape may rise;
Fear may unveil our eyes.
For know you not what curse of blight would fall
Upon a land lorn of the sweet sky races
Who day and night keep ward and seneschal
Upon the treasury of the planted spaces?
Then would the locust have his fill,
And the blind worm lay tithe,
The unfed stones rot in the listless mill,
The sound of grinding cease.
No yearning gold would whisper to the scythe,
Hunger at last would prove us of one blood,
The shores of dream be drowned in tides of need,
Horribly would the whole earth be at peace.
The burden of the grasshopper indeed
Weigh down the green corn and the tender bud,
The plague of Egypt fall upon the wheat,
And the shrill nit would batten in the heat.

But you, O poor of deeds and rich of breath,
Whose eyes have made our eyes a hue abhorred,
Red, eager aids of aid-unneeding Death,
Hunters before the Lord,
If on the flinted marge about your souls
In vain the heaving tide of mourning rolls,
If from your trails unto the crimson goals
The weeper and the weeping must depart,

If lust of blood come on you like a fiery dart
And darken all the dark autumnal air,
Then, then — be fair.
Pluck a young ash tree or a sapling yew
And at the root end fix an iron thorn,
Then forth with rocking laughter of the horn
And passing, with no belling retinue,
All timorous, lesser sippers of the dew,
Seek out some burly guardian of the hills
And set your urgent thew against his thew.
Then shall the hidden wisdoms and the wills
Strive, and bear witness to the trees and clods
How one has dumb lore of the rocks and swales
And one has reason like unto the gods.
Then shall the lagging righteousness ensue,
The powers at last be equal in the scales,
And the man's club and the beast's claw be flails
To winnow the unworthy of the two.
Then on the earth, in the sky and the heavenly court
That broods behind it,
Justice shall be awakened and aware,
Then those who go forth greatly, seeking sport,
Shall doubtless find it,
And all things be fair.

Ridgely Torrence.

A VAGABOND SONG

There is something in the autumn that is native to
my blood —
Touch of manner, hint of mood;
And my heart is like a rhyme,
With the yellow and the purple and the crimson
keeping time.

The scarlet of the maples can shake me like a cry
Of bugles going by.
And my lonely spirit thrills
To see the frosty asters like a smoke upon the hills.

There is something in October sets the gypsy blood
astir;
We must rise and follow her,
When from every hill of flame
She calls and calls each vagabond by name.

Bliss Carman.

SOMEWHERE

THE weasel thieves in silver suit,
The rabbit runs in gray;
And Pan takes up his frosty flute
To pipe the cold away.

The flocks are folded, boughs are bare,
The salmon take the sea;
And O my fair, would I somewhere
Might house my heart with thee!

John Vance Cheney.

"FROST TO-NIGHT"

APPLE-GREEN west and an orange bar,
And the crystal eye of a lone, one star . . .
And, "Child, take the shears and cut what you will,
Frost to-night — so clear and dead-still."

Then, I sally forth, half sad, half proud,
And I come to the velvet, imperial crowd,
The wine-red, the gold, the crimson, the pied, —
The dahlias that reign by the garden-side.

The dahlias I might not touch till to-night!
A gleam of the shears in the fading light,
And I gathered them all, — the splendid throng,
And in one great sheaf I bore them along.

. . . .

In my garden of Life with its all-late flowers
I heed a Voice in the shrinking hours:
"Frost to-night — so clear and dead-still" . . .
Half sad, half proud, my arms I fill.

Edith M. Thomas.

UNDER ARCTURUS

I

"I BELT the morn with ribboned mist;
With baldricked blue I gird the noon,
And dusk with purple, crimson-kissed,
White-buckled with the hunter's-moon.

"These follow me," the Season says:
"Mine is the frost-pale hand that packs
Their scrips, and speeds them on their ways,
With gypsy gold that weighs their backs."

II

A daybreak horn the Autumn blows,
As with a sun-tanned hand he parts

Wet boughs whereon the berry glows;
And at his feet the red fox starts.

The leafy leash that holds his hounds
Is loosed; and all the noonday hush
Is startled; and the hillside sounds
Behind the fox's bounding brush.

When red dusk makes the western sky
A fire-lit window through the firs,
He stoops to see the red fox die
Among the chestnut's broken burrs.

Then fanfaree and fanfaree,
His bugle sounds; the world below
Grows hushed to hear; and two or three
Soft stars dream through the afterglow.

III

Like some black host the shadows fall,
And blackness camps among the trees;
Each wildwood road, a Goblin Hall,
Grows populous with mysteries.

Night comes with brows of ragged storm,
And limbs of writhen cloud and mist;
The rain-wind hangs upon his arm
Like some wild girl who cries unkissed.

By his gaunt hands the leaves are shed
In headlong troops and nightmare herds;
And, like a witch who calls the dead,
The hill-stream whirls with foaming words.

Then all is sudden silence and
  Dark fear — like his who cannot see,
Yet hears, lost in a haunted land,
  Death rattling on a gallow's-tree.

IV

The days approach again; the days
  Whose mantles stream, whose sandals drag,
When in the haze by puddled ways
  The gnarled thorn seems a crooked hag.

When rotting orchards reek with rain;
  And woodlands crumble, leaf and log;
And in the drizzling yard again
  The gourd is tagged with points of fog.

Now let me seat my soul among
  The woods' dim dreams, and come in touch
With melancholy, sad of tongue
  And sweet, who says so much, so much.

Madison Cawein.

THE RECESSIONAL

Now along the solemn heights
Fade the Autumn's altar-lights;
  Down the great earth's glimmering chancel
Glide the days and nights.

Little kindred of the grass,
Like a shadow in a glass
  Falls the dark and falls the stillness;
We must rise and pass.

We must rise and follow, wending
Where the nights and days have ending, —
  Pass in order pale and slow
Unto sleep extending.

Little brothers of the clod,
Soul of fire and seed of sod,
  We must fare into the silence
At the knees of God.

Little comrades of the sky,
Wing to wing we wander by,
  Going, going, going, going,
Softly as a sigh.

Hark, the moving shapes confer,
Globe of dew and gossamer,
  Fading and ephemeral spirits
In the dusk astir.

Moth and blossom, blade and bee,
Worlds must go as well as we,
  In the long procession joining
Mount and star and sea.

Toward the shadowy brink we climb
Where the round year rolls sublime,
  Rolls, and drops, and falls forever
In the vast of time.

Like a plummet plunging deep
Past the utmost reach of sleep,
  Till remembrance has no longer
Care to laugh or weep.

Charles G. D. Roberts.

I KNOW NOT WHY

I LIFT mine eyes against the sky,
The clouds are weeping, so am I;
I lift mine eyes again on high,
The sun is smiling, so am I.
Why do I smile? Why do I weep?
I do not know; it lies too deep.

I hear the winds of autumn sigh,
They break my heart, they make me cry;
I hear the birds of lovely spring,
My hopes revive, I help them sing.
Why do I sing? Why do I cry?
It lies so deep, I know not why.

Morris Rosenfeld.

WINTER SLEEP

I KNOW it must be winter (though I sleep) —
I know it must be winter, for I dream
I dip my bare feet in the running stream,
And flowers are many, and the grass grows deep.

I know I must be old (how age deceives!)
I know I must be old, for, all unseen,
My heart grows young, as autumn fields grow green,
When late rains patter on the falling sheaves.

I know I must be tired (and tired souls err) —
I know I must be tired, for all my soul
To deeds of daring beats a glad, faint roll,
As storms the riven pine to music stir.

I know I must be dying (Death draws near) —
I know I must be dying, for I crave
Life — life, strong life, and think not of the grave,
And turf-bound silence, in the frosty year.

Edith M. Thomas

TRYSTE NOËL

The Ox he openeth wide the Doore,
And from the Snowe he calls her inne,
And he hath seen her Smile therefor,
Our Ladye without Sinne.
Now soon from Sleep
A Starre shall leap,
And soone arrive both King and Hinde:
Amen, Amen:
But O, the Place co'd I but finde!

The Ox hath hush'd his voyce and bent
Trewe eyes of Pitty ore the Mow,
And on his lovelie Neck, forspent,
The Blessed layes her Browe.
Around her feet
Full Warme and Sweete
His bowerie Breath doth meeklie dwell:
Amen, Amen:
But sore am I with Vaine Travèl!

The Ox is host in Judah stall
And Host of more than onelie one.
For close she gathereth withal
Our Lorde her littel Sonne.

Glad Hinde and King
Their Gyfte may bring,
But wo'd to-night my Teares were there,
Amen, Amen:
Between her Bosom and His hayre!

Louise Imogen Guiney.

HORA CHRISTI

Sweet is the time for joyous folk
Of gifts and minstrelsy;
Yet I, O lowly-hearted One,
Crave but Thy company.
On lonesome road, beset with dread,
My questing lies afar.
I have no light, save in the east
The gleaming of Thy star.

In cloistered aisles they keep to-day
Thy feast, O living Lord!
With pomp of banner, pride of song,
And stately sounding word.
Mute stand the kings of power and place,
While priests of holy mind
Dispense Thy blessed heritage
Of peace to all mankind.

I know a spot where budless twigs
Are bare above the snow,
And where sweet winter-loving birds
Flit softly to and fro;
There with the sun for altar-fire,
The earth for kneeling-place,

The gentle air for chorister,
  Will I adore Thy face.

Loud, underneath the great blue sky,
  My heart shall pæan sing,
The gold and myrrh of meekest love
  Mine only offering.
Bliss of Thy birth shall quicken me;
  And for Thy pain and dole
Tears are but vain, so I will keep
  The silence of the soul.

Alice Brown.

A PARTING GUEST

WHAT delightful hosts are they —
  Life and Love!
Lingeringly I turn away,
  This late hour, yet glad enough
They have not withheld from me
  Their high hospitality.
So, with face lit with delight
  And all gratitude, I stay
  Yet to press their hands and say,
"Thanks. — So fine a time! Good night."

James Whitcomb Riley.

INDEX OF AUTHORS

INDEX OF FIRST LINES

The Riverside Press

CAMBRIDGE . MASSACHUSETTS

U . S . A

www.ingramcontent.com/pod-product-compliance
Lightning Source LLC
LaVergne TN
LVHW011202110826
845150LV00006B/1293

* 9 7 8 1 4 2 5 5 7 2 4 5 7 *